WORKING
EFFECTIVELY
WITH
GRADUATE
ASSISTANTS

WORKING
EFFECTIVELY
WITH
GRADUATE
ASSISTANTS

JODY D. NYQUIST
DONALD H. WULFF

SAGE Publications
International Educational and Professional Publisher
Thousand Oaks   London   New Delhi

For information address:

SAGE Publications, Inc.
2455 Teller Road
Thousand Oaks, California 91320
E-mail: order@sagepub.com

SAGE Publications Ltd.
6 Bonhill Street
London EC2A 4PU
United Kingdom

SAGE Publications India Pvt. Ltd.
M-32 Market
Greater Kailash I
New Delhi 110 048 India

Printed in the United States of America

Library of Congress Cataloging-in-Publication Data

Nyquist, Jody D.
    Working effectively with graduate assistants / authors, Jody D. Nyquist and Donald H. Wulff.
        p.   cm.
    Includes bibliographical references.
    ISBN 0-8039-5313-5 (cloth). — ISBN 0-8039-5314-3 (pbk.)
    1. Graduate teaching assistants—United States.   2. College teachers—United States.   I. Wulff, Donald H.   II. Title.
LB2335.4.N98   1996
378.1′25—dc20   95-32508

This book is printed on acid-free paper.

96 97 98 99 10 9 8 7 6 5 4 3 2 1

Sage Project Editor: Christina M. Hill

Contents

To Jo Sprague, colleague, friend, and TA supervisor par excellence, whose influence on our understanding of the development and refinement of TA/RA preparation has been substantial, and whose wisdom permeates our thinking, and thus this volume.

Acknowledgments

We wish to express our appreciation to the numerous individuals who assisted in the completion of this volume. First, we want to express gratitude to the many faculty supervisors and TAs who, over the years, have contributed, either explicitly or implicitly, to our knowledge and understanding of the supervision of TAs and RAs. During our combined nearly 40 years of experience in this area, we have learned much from faculty and TAs who have willingly given their time and openly described their concerns, approaches, and strategies. The contributions of many such individuals are reflected in this volume. We are particularly grateful to Professors Barbara Krieger-Brockett and Eric Stuve of the Department of Chemical Engineering for their ideas and innovative approaches to supervision.

We are indebted to Gabriele Bauer, who has authored Chapter 7 on international TAs and whose experience as an ITA and expertise as a researcher focused on ITA issues make her an extremely valuable collaborator. Dr. Bauer offers her special thanks to the international teaching assistants at the University of Washington for sharing their stories with her. She appreciates their commitment to being effective instructors and all they have taught her about their instructional roles, rewards, and challenges.

We also wish to express our appreciation to our colleagues at the Center for Instructional Development and Research: to the CIDR consultants who, over the years, have challenged, supported, and expanded our thinking about the issues of TA/RA supervision; and to all of the support staff who have assisted, particularly our administrative assistant, Brenda Kelly, for keeping us organized and on track, and Madelle Quiring, secretary, for her tireless efforts in transcribing, word processing, and proofreading. We are blessed with a superb support staff, and we could not have reached the completion of this project without their efforts. We extend special thanks to Julie Chiapelone, research assistant, for interviewing supervisors, pursuing resources, and providing feedback as we progressed. Her interview data were crucial to our conceptualization of the book, and her professionalism and conscientiousness greatly reduced the complexity of our task.

Finally, we wish to express our appreciation to Sage Publications for believing we had something to say on this topic and for supporting us in getting it said. Particularly, we wish to acknowledge the following editors: Mitch Allen, whose patience is extraordinary, and whose many insights enhanced the volume; to Frances Borghi for moving the project through its various permutations to completion; and to Peter Labella, who saw the potential of publishing these ideas as a separate volume. Their contributions have been meaningful and have provided more than editorial advice.

We set out to write a volume that would help you to reflect on the issues of supervision, aid you in developing your own supervisory style, and provide you with specific ideas and strategies. We know there is yet much to be learned about supervision as practitioners and researchers systematically examine various approaches for preparing graduate students for their current responsibilities as teaching assistants and research assistants, and for their future professional lives. We invite and welcome your participation in the conversation.

JDN
DHW

1

Understanding the Challenges of Working With Graduate Teaching Assistants and Graduate Research Assistants

We are assuming that in turning to this book you may be in one of several positions:

- You are a newly appointed assistant professor at a university with a graduate program and are just beginning to supervise graduate students who will act as teaching assistants (TAs) or research assistants (RAs).
- You have recently moved from a college or university department without a Ph.D. program and, although you have taught many years at the university level, you have not directed graduate students.
- You have been directing graduate students for a while and are interested in new ideas.
- You are a chair or university administrator interested in ways of assisting new faculty to move easily into graduate student supervision.
- You are a graduate student interested in what your supervisor should be doing.
- You are a graduate program advisor and are interested in assisting your colleagues to direct the work of TAs and RAs more effectively.
- You are simply curious about the topic.

Clearly, faculty supervise TAs and RAs for different reasons, with different levels of commitment and different types of preparation for the role. We know there is great diversity in your individual needs as supervisors because supervising graduate students is very personal and idiosyncratic. What works for one person may not be effective for another.

We also know from our research, however, that most supervisors rely on their personal, but often limited, experience as their only guide in the area of graduate student supervision. Graduate student interviewees on our campus, both TAs and RAs, report that they either emulate their own supervisors' styles or try to treat their students in a manner that is opposite from the supervision that they experienced. Supervisors tend to do the same, using their own supervisors as models to be imitated or avoided.

Whatever experience you may bring to the role of TA/RA supervisor, you, on a particular day, begin this responsibility. You may be supervising only one teaching assistant or researcher, or you may be responsible for directing a multisectioned or large course with many TAs, or you may be directing a large grant with numerous RAs. Each of these supervisory positions requires that you assume a multidimensional role that includes being a manager, an educational role model, and a professional mentor (Sprague & Nyquist, 1989).

With this variety of roles in mind, we have based the book on two major premises:

- Good supervision does not simply happen, but rather emerges as a result of systematic thinking and planning that you can do regardless of your level of supervisory experience, your discipline, the number of teaching assistants and research assistants with whom you work, or the roles they play in instruction or research.
- Working with teaching assistants and research assistants is an intellectually stimulating role that not only prepares the next generation of university teaching scholars/researchers and professionals outside the academy, but also provides an important learning opportunity for supervisors.

Throughout this book, we have used the term *teaching assistant* broadly. TAs are graduate students who have instructional responsibilities in which they interact with undergraduates, either orally or in writing. TAs may have instructional responsibilities that range from grading tests and papers, to having office hours, to leading laboratories and discussion sections, to assuming full responsibility for a course. Each of these responsibilities requires specific skills and certain kinds of supervision. Our use of the term *research assistant* is likewise inclusive. RAs are graduate students who are funded but not yet working on a specific research project or are those who are funded to work with a professor in a specific research project/program or are graduate students who have received funding for their own research.

We are committed to assisting supervisors of both TAs and RAs to view supervision as an intellectually engaging activity and not simply as an administrative headache. We know that faculty members are sometimes less likely to view the supervision of *TAs* as a career goal, whereas most look forward to supervising *RAs* because of the close, highly personalized mentoring and intellectual growth that often occurs during a shared research project. In either case, professional competence involves making unique judgments about completely novel cases, and beginners need to systematically develop the ability to do so. Assisting graduate students to become independent, reflective, and collaborative problem solvers in both teaching and research is an exciting enterprise worth our time, expertise, and best efforts.

To assist you with this important enterprise, we have relied on our collective 40 years of work with TAs and RAs and supervisors in a variety of disciplines on a number of different campuses to provide not only discussion of the important issues, but also specific suggestions, tips, strategies, approaches, and resources for you to consider as you think about your specific supervisory needs. We have organized the book to address the following:

- Supervisory relationships with TAs and RAs (Chapter 2)
- Developmental stages of TAs or RAs (Chapter 3)
- Special challenges for TAs (Chapter 4)
- Preparation of TAs for typical instructional roles (Chapter 5)
- Preparation of RAs for various research responsibilities (Chapter 6)
- Special challenges of working with international teaching assistants (ITAs) (Chapter 7)

- Assessment of TAs/RAs (Chapter 8)
- A framework for supervisory action (Chapter 9)
- A print and video list of resources (Chapter 10)

We believe that TA/RA supervision is a noble calling and hope that the information addressed in this volume will help you reflect upon your role as supervisor of TAs and RAs. Providing TAs/RAs with systematic, incremental opportunities for gaining competence not only contributes to the professional development of the next generation, but also allows you to approach this responsibility in meaningful ways rather than as a set of disorganized, unfulfilling managerial acts. We hope this book will contribute to your ability to approach this challenge with excitement, energy, and insight.

2

Establishing Supervisory Relationships With Graduate Teaching Assistants and Graduate Research Assistants

The quality of your supervision lies in the relationships you develop with the teaching assistants (TAs) and research assistants (RAs) you supervise. Those relationships will depend jointly on awareness of your own needs and expectations as a supervisor and on understanding the levels of background and experience of the TAs/RAs. You will find, as our work suggests, that graduate students come to you at varying stages in their development. Trying to group them into three levels sometimes helps to work with them. For example, some graduate students—usually those just beginning their graduate work—are often in the stage labeled Senior Learner because they have actually been selected for their demonstrated competence as learners rather than as teachers or researchers. Those TAs or RAs who have some experience as graduate students may be at a second level called Colleague-in-Training. Finally, experienced TAs/RAs are often more like colleagues than subordinates, a stage referred to as Junior Colleague.

Although you will always be working with the TA or RA as employer-employee, this kind of relationship may be more dominant, for instance, in the beginning. When you work with TAs and RAs in the colleague-in-training stage, the relationship may focus primarily on advising or on role-modeling effective behaviors and approaches to teaching and research. When the graduate students become junior colleagues, the relationship may be more collaborative—like that of peers. At different times, then, depending on your needs and the needs of individual graduate students, you will fulfill a variety of roles in your overall relationship with the TAs and RAs. We can view the major roles as those of manager, model, and mentor.[1]

Manager

Often, the beginning role you will assume, particularly with new, less experienced TAs or RAs, or senior learners, will require managerial skills. The management role includes personnel duties. You will have to require TAs/RAs to meet certain standards of excellence; you will appoint, motivate, coordinate, monitor, and, hopefully infrequently, dismiss your TAs/RAs. The manager role is particularly challenging because it requires skills that many of us have not necessarily developed. Although most of us manage our lives as faculty in effective ways, we are, by the definition of a faculty member/researcher, less likely to have experience with managerial tasks. To assist you, we have developed some basic management guidelines.

Establish the Supervisory Relationship Early. The most successful managers plan ahead, preparing both themselves and their constituents for their managerial role. Because graduate students accept responsibilities more willingly and more successfully if they have forewarning, you can send a letter and materials before the graduate students arrive on campus. The letter can describe the instructional research assignment and send a message about your willingness to assist. In addition, you might include materials about training, textbooks and materials for courses in which the TAs will be involved, or background on the research area with which RAs will assist.

- It is especially important in such early contacts to inform the TAs/RAs about times that you want them to participate in activities before the autumn term begins so that they can arrive in time to take care of the logistics of housing, bank accounts, and so on in advance of the planned activities. Remember, however, that other departmental representatives, such as the chair or the graduate program advisor, also may be corresponding with the graduate students. You will want to check that there is no duplication or inconsistent information being sent from various sources. There may even be ways to coordinate or combine mailings. If you cannot contact the students before they arrive on campus, it is imperative that you interact with them as soon as possible after their arrival.
- A short initial meeting in which you provide information about the job and your willingness to support their efforts can go a long way in establishing the relationship.
- By distributing appropriate print materials at an initial meeting, you can keep the initial contact short and focused.
- If you do not have a departmental or university handbook that you can distribute, you can prepare a packet of materials with useful information (see Appendix A for suggestions of materials to include).

It is this kind of planning that can get your supervisory relationship off to a good start and make your managerial role more pleasant for everyone involved.

Clarify Expectations. Good managers are explicit about what they expect from their employees.

- One way that you can enhance the relationship with the TAs/ RAs that you supervise is to make sure they have a clear understanding of your supervisory expectations. A first step is to make sure that they understand the requirements and responsibilities for the jobs they are to perform. Provide details of the job assignment, the tasks that go with the job, the skills needed for the job, the kind of assistance that will be provided, and the procedures you and/or the department will use to assess their effectiveness.
- A second important way to clarify expectations is to make sure TAs/RAs have information about relevant departmental and institutional policies and procedures. Providing this information often requires not only

that the information be given to them and discussed but that they be given appropriate strategies for dealing with violations of the policies or procedures. Thus, for example, TAs may need to know that they cannot automatically fail a student on an assignment for cheating, but they will also need ways to talk to students about the cheating. RAs, for instance, may need to know of any special policies related to the use of laboratories or to the publishing of information generated through collaborative research. As they are developing a variety of relationships on campus, it is also important that all graduate students understand policies related to issues such as sexual harassment. At the minimum, they need to understand the appropriate channels for dealing with such issues. Also, you will want to establish expectations about what issues and problems should be discussed with you before they are taken to other faculty or the chair of the department.

- If you have particular needs or managerial idiosyncrasies that you want TAs/RAs to be aware of, those also can be made explicit. It is usually helpful to provide a brief rationale, giving reasons why you choose to manage as you do. In addition, it is useful to talk to the TAs/RAs about what seems to work best. Thus, you can couch some of your own needs in statements like, "Although I encourage you to come directly to me in cases that demand immediate attention, I want you to know that I work best if you set up appointments ahead of time" or "I work best if I can help you deal with a problem in its initial stages while we can still be proactive rather than after it has gone so far that we can only react" or "Because I believe we work best when we collaborate, I will be asking all of you to participate in weekly meetings in which we discuss our instructional or research issues as a group." Finally, it will help the TAs/RAs if you can provide explicit information about what they can expect when they meet with you, either about their own problems related to policies and procedures or about problems they have encountered with students, other researchers, graduate students, and so on. For example, it might be appropriate to explain that you will spend time listening to the issue(s), that you will provide specific strategies to help them resolve the issue(s), or that you will direct them to appropriate resources.

Be Responsive to the Needs of TAs/RAs. Just as you bring a unique style and specific needs to the supervisory relationship, RAs/TAs also bring specific needs, expectations, and styles. Thus, to enhance your relationships with TAs/RAs, you might ask the individual graduate students what kind of supervision they think works best for them. Some may suggest that they need to be monitored closely; others might indicate that they prefer autonomy or independence. Although initially you may monitor them closely to determine that their choices for supervision work for both of you, giving the TAs/RAs some freedom of choice can be helpful in developing trusting relationships that will enhance your work as a manager.

Focus on Both the Instructional Task and the Interpersonal Part of the Relationship. The role of the manager is particularly difficult because, more than other roles, it requires a careful balancing. On one hand, the TAs/RAs may need strong guidance for the task because they are new to the instructional or research role. On the other hand, as new graduate students, many of them have interpersonal needs for empathy and support. For you, then, the key, especially with less experienced TAs/RAs, is to manage with a balance of focus on the task and the interpersonal needs.

For a number of reasons, it is important to focus on the task of helping the TAs/RAs with their roles:

- *The quality of their work has ramifications for you, the department, and the university.* TAs, of course, are providing education for undergraduates. Hopefully, graduate instructors who are carefully prepared are in a better position to provide high-quality instruction to the students they teach. The work of RAs affects the quality of your research and has the potential to put the department in either a favorable or unfavorable position.
- *The actions of the TAs/RAs have legal ramifications for you and the institution.* When TAs/RAs are fulfilling their assigned instructional roles or using university facilities to conduct research, individual departments and the university are legally responsible for the way they interact with undergraduate students, other graduate students, faculty, and administrators.
- *As an experienced instructor, you have an ethical responsibility to help others prepare as future colleagues and professionals.* The graduate students are entitled to the best preparation they can receive for both their present and their future roles and responsibilities.

While focusing on the task of preparing TAs/RAs, it is also important to remember, as a manager, that successful relationships involve interpersonal dynamics between the supervisor and the TAs/RAs. Often, graduate students enter programs with needs for emotional support and for evidence that there is concern for their survival. Many are dealing with relationships as parents, as significant others, and/or as citizens. In particular, new graduate students can experience the feelings of being incapable or unprepared, or of not measuring up to the rest of the group. Such self-perceptions can lead to problems with confidence and, ultimately, with performance. In the managerial role, you can provide important validation for graduate students in their new roles.

Address Explicitly the Tension Between Being a Graduate Student and Being an Employee. The best managers attempt to ward off common problems before they arise.

- You can make your managerial duties easier if you acknowledge up front that many graduate students face the ongoing issues of how to fulfill the dual, and often conflicting, roles of graduate student and instructor/researcher. We know many successful supervisors who talk to the TAs/RAs about the tension as a natural prelude to the balancing of teaching, research, and service that they will engage in as professionals. For example, if you view their primary role as that of graduate students whose academic responsibilities are foremost, tell them so. If you expect the TAs or RAs to spend equal amounts of time on their instructional or research responsibilities and their graduate studies, clarify how you view those responsibilities. Then reassure them that you will be willing to help them when they are struggling to achieve the appropriate balance.
- You can also address the tension by encouraging ongoing relationships in which the experienced graduate students mentor the less experienced students or by conducting a session in which experienced graduate students discuss their initial tensions and how they dealt with them. Recently, in one department, we divided the graduate students into small groups based on their responsibilities and had them meet briefly with the experienced graduate students who had fulfilled similar roles.

The experienced TAs/RAs provided straightforward strategies to help the newer TAs/RAs deal with the tensions. But the most useful outcome of the session was that the experienced TAs/RAs put to rest many of the initial concerns by explaining that they worried more about the conflicting roles than necessary and that some of the worst parts of the tension were diminished as they became accustomed to their roles.

The more you are able to clarify their roles, your expectations, and your managerial style, the more solid your relationship with TAs/RAs will be. Talking at length about the tension and emphasizing the need for TAs/RAs to meet expectations, however, can exacerbate the fear of failure. Thus, you need to stress that the TAs/RAs have already proven that they can be successful and have been selected for graduate study on that basis. So, the department has a commitment to them and will work with them to help them deal with the tensions they experience. It is important in your managerial role to let the TAs/RAs know that although you expect them to fulfill their responsibilities, you want them to be successful and that you will support them when they are having difficulty as well as when they are succeeding.

Educational Model

Another supervisory role that you may assume is that of educational model. At some stage of our development in any activity, we learn by watching others. When TAs/RAs reach this point, they are ready for new ideas and creative approaches. They can now do the basic job, but they want to think about innovative ways to teach, generate data, or formulate hypotheses. They are, in essence, in a discovery phase. You then become a model for them. In this role, there are also a number of guidelines to consider.

Act in the Ways You Want the TAs/RAs to Act. We recently asked TAs from a variety of disciplines to tell us stories about incidents that strongly influenced the kind of teacher they are. One TA told a story about a college professor who was so good about encouraging both men and women in a physics class that she decided to go on to study physics. Another talked about a seventh-grade teacher "who really cared about our learning and made learning fun." We heard time and again about individuals, especially teachers—from the early years all the way through undergraduate education—who had in some way influenced the TAs. More important, however, the stories revealed that in many cases, model instructors never knew they were serving in such an important role. Certainly, in the stories TAs told us, there was no indication that either the instructors or the students were aware at the time that the instructors were serving as role models. Thus, your behaviors can influence TAs/RAs, even when you may not be aware of such possibilities. If you want TAs to learn to ask probing questions in order to encourage students to think critically about new information, for example, then provide opportunities for them to see you asking such questions. If you think that it is important that RAs allow time for reflection and avoid last minute data analysis and interpretation, then demonstrate those behaviors as you work with RAs.

Use a Variety of Ways of Teaching/Researching. One way to assist TAs/RAs is to demonstrate an array of methods so that they can see varied approaches in action. For example, you can provide TAs with opportunities to see you use a variety of planning approaches, different methods of imparting information to students, and tests that measure student learning in varied ways. Similarly, when possible, you should show RAs multiple ways of collecting and recording data, interpreting results, generating alternative hypotheses, and displaying results. Such variation reflects a broader conceptualization of their development beyond their immediate assignments and helps them recognize that teaching and research do not have to be done in a singular way and that TAs/RAs can choose from many options the ones that fit their own emerging styles.

It is also important to realize that you do not have to be the only model for the TAs/RAs. In those instances in which you feel you cannot provide the variety with which the TAs/RAs might benefit, you might:

- Encourage TAs to observe in each other's classes or in the classes of other professors who use a variety of styles.

- Provide access to video playback so that TAs can watch samples of teaching on videotape in a setting where they can play back and discuss different instructional behaviors.
- Encourage RAs to observe or talk to experienced RAs and other faculty who use different approaches or to consult published research that addresses similar topics in different ways.

Demonstrate How You Think About Teaching or Research. If TAs/RAs are to learn from you, such learning can be enhanced if you not only show them instructional or research behaviors but also demonstrate how you think about the instructional or research process. Obviously, this is the information to which the TAs and RAs do not have direct access. Yet it is some of the most potentially valuable information they can obtain.

When you are planning a lesson, a course, or a research project, you might include TAs/RAs and talk to them, not only about what steps you are going through but also what is going on in your mind. As you are being reflective about your teaching/research, the TAs/RAs also can be reflective about why you made your choices and how similar choices might be incorporated in their own work. You might also play back a videotape of your own teaching or use your own research log to show how you were making decisions as you worked. Then provide plenty of opportunities for questions and reflection. The TAs/RAs will need opportunities to probe your thinking, and you will need to be open to their inquiry. Either when you meet with TAs/RAs in group meetings or as you work with them individually, you can demonstrate by saying, "Let me show you how I might think about that" or "Together, let's think about how we could apply to this particular case the basic steps of analysis that we have discussed."

Mentor

As the relationship between you and your TAs/RAs develops, you typically will become their mentor, usually when they are able to interact with you more as a peer. This is an important stage for the TAs/RAs because it provides an opportunity for them to learn collegial roles, to ask questions, seek information, express concerns, or suggest ideas in ways that they would not when working with you primarily as a manager or a model. We offer the following guidelines to assist you in the mentoring role.

Be Collaborative. If you think of your supervision as preparing TAs/RAs for professional responsibilities after they graduate, you must also think about the collaborative skills that TAs/RAs need to learn. Unfortunately, one of the biggest issues that TAs/RAs have expressed to us about this stage of their development is the lack of supervisory openness to a collaborative relationship. For example, TAs perceive that when a mentoring role is often appropriate for their supervisors, the supervisors become threatened by the increasing symmetry of the relationship. When TAs encounter this kind of reluctance, their development is impeded and they resort to previous levels of development, most often turning to other TAs for mentoring relationships. They lose the valuable opportunity to refine their instructional knowledge and skills by working with an experienced professional. This same kind of constriction is applicable to the researcher role in which the graduate researcher does not feel comfortable raising questions or offering alternative viewpoints, or feels that he or she is simply serving as an extra "hand" for the project. The key for the supervisor is to recognize the need for TAs/RAs to experience meaningful mentoring relationships with their supervisors and to determine how mentoring roles can best be incorporated into their own supervisory style.

You can encourage collaboration and reinforce TAs' and RAs' confidence in their own abilities/perspectives by:

- Sending messages that you are open to differing perspectives. Ask TAs/RAs to suggest different ways that you might teach a concept or approach a research question.
- Inviting input about your own teaching/research from TAs/RAs. By the time they are ready for collaborative relationships with you, they should have developed their own areas of expertise.
- Mentoring the TAs/RAs in small groups where they can learn collectively from you and from each other.

View the TAs/RAs as Decision Makers. By this point in their development, TAs/RAs will begin to realize that there are a variety of ways of teaching/researching, and their own style will have begun to emerge. As a mentor, you can help them realize that teaching and conducting research are decision-making processes that happen in a particular moment. From the planning right on into the many decisions one makes while teaching, instructors/researchers are continually choosing one approach, one method, one idea, or one conclusion over another. You can listen to their ideas, provide feedback and additional insights, and help them think about the implications of their decisions. Yet at this point in their development, it is important for you to realize that they can learn much by taking your input but setting their own priorities, approaching instructional and research tasks in their own way, and learning from their own successes and failures.

Provide Ample Opportunities for Dialogue. The kind of learning experience provided by a mentoring relationship requires that TAs/RAs and supervisors talk to each other frequently. To think of the mentoring process as dialogue has specific implications for your supervisory role. As a mentor, your role shifts from that of expert having all the answers to that of "sounding board" and resource. Thus, when you are in dialogue with TAs/RAs, you should find yourself listening more to their ideas and asking lots of questions that will help them be reflective about their decisions as opposed to telling and showing them what they ought to be doing.

As a mentor, you will soon realize that both you and the TAs/RAs are busy. Busy professors often handle their relentless schedules by privatizing their work. To avoid similar privatization by TAs/RAs, you might:

- Help them build into their schedules time to talk about teaching/research.
- Provide stimuli for good discussion (For TAs, you might also use other sources of input, such as a classroom observation, a set of student ratings, or a videotape of a TA teaching as an impetus for discussing teaching in a mentoring relationship. Similarly, previous research or the work of experienced RAs might provide a stimulus for your supervision of RAs).
- Be accessible during set, agreed-upon times to answer questions and help them with instructional or research problems.

• Provide opportunities for them to meet with you during the design phase of courses, the planning of instructional activities, or the designing and implementing of research.

A key to successful supervision, then, is to think seriously about the best ways to fulfill the various supervisory roles. In this chapter, we have identified three of those supervisory roles and provided some suggestions for fulfilling each of them. The suggested activities may seem like a lot for a single supervisor; however, you must realize that although you may be moving back and forth between the roles, you may not be engaged in all three roles simultaneously. Rather, you will change from role to role depending on a number of other important factors. Among those factors—and one that we discuss in the next chapter—is the idea that TAs/RAs move through stages in developing their ability to teach or conduct research and thus require you to be a manager, model, or mentor at different times in their development.

Note

1. The idea of using the roles of manager, educational model, and mentor to address the needs of graduate students as senior learners, colleagues in training, and junior colleagues was originally discussed by Sprague and Nyquist (1989).

APPENDIX A

Materials to Include in an Introductory Packet for TAs/RAs

- Letter(s) of Welcome From the Chair and You
- Information on the University or Department
    Brief Background Information
    List of Names of Relevant Personnel
    List of Names of Other New Graduate Students
- Campus Maps
- Information on Housing/Banking, Getting Settled
- University and Departmental Policies Related to the Terms of Appointment
    Definition of the TA/RA Role in Your Department
    Explanation of How TAs/RAs Are Chosen and Assigned
    Length of Appointment
    Conditions of Renewal, Promotion, and Termination
    Conduct, Sexual Harassment, Diversity, and Grievances
    Hours of Work
    Expectation for Initial and Ongoing Training
    Salary and Benefits
    Relevant Fee Waivers
    Academic Responsibilities
    A Summary of Major Components of the Assessment Process (see Chapter 8)
- Schedule of Initial Training Activities
- An Academic Calendar
- List of Campus and Departmental Resources
    Graduate Study
    Teaching
    Research

3

Recognizing and Adapting to Stages of Graduate Teaching Assistants' and Graduate Research Assistants' Development

As many researchers have been discovering (Austin, 1992, 1993; Boice, 1991, 1992; Chism, 1988, 1993; Fink, 1984; Grossman, 1992; Hunt, 1971; Jenrette, 1993; Kagan, 1988; Kugel, 1993; Nyquist, Skow, Sprague, & Wulff, 1991; Nyquist & Sprague, 1992; Nyquist & Wulff, 1992; Sorcinelli & Austin, 1992; Sprague & Nyquist, 1989, 1991; Sprinthall & Thies-Sprinthall, 1983; Stoltenberg, 1981; Tierney & Rhoads, 1994; Weimer, 1993a), beginning faculty members move through a set of developmental stages that, if completed, allow them to become professional, confident problem solvers, effective in their interactions over content and productive in their research. To supervise teaching assistants/research assistants (TAs/RAs) who are moving from novice to professional levels, you should take time to think about where the individuals you supervise are in the developmental phase of *aspiring* teacher/scholar.

The three phases of graduate student development suggested by Sprague and Nyquist (1989) give us a place to begin to identify where your students may be. As explained in Chapter 2 of this the three phases, Senior Learner, Colleague-in-Training, and Jun. Colleague, require slightly different leadership from you in your roles as manager, educational model, and mentor. The obvious question is, How do you identify at what stage your graduate students are in such a developmental framework so that you can adapt your supervision to match their needs?

Although we are really at the beginning of actually testing the framework (Sprague & Nyquist, 1991), we believe that you can think about your TAs/RAs along at least four dimensions to determine where they may be at the present time—their concerns, their discourse, their attitudes toward authority and toward their students as represented in Figure 3.1. Development is not usually linear. In fact, we believe that growth is typically spiral. In addition, aspiring teacher/researchers may be more developed on one dimension than another, and at times, they may revert to a previous stage, particularly when confronted with a new experience.

We believe, however, that systematically observing and listening to the TAs and RAs with whom you work will provide you sufficient information about where they are in their development and what leadership and interventions are most appropriate. Ask yourself four questions: What are my graduate students concerned about related to their teaching and research responsibilities? How do my graduate students talk about our discipline? How do my graduate students relate to authority—primarily to their dissertation supervisors and to me as their TA/RA supervisor? And finally, how do my TAs seem to relate to their students? Answers to these questions will provide some insight as to where your graduate students might be along these four dimensions and thus suggest appropriate levels of supervision.

Beginning Teachers'/
Researchers' Concerns

Graduate Student Instructors. Based on considerable research (Bauer, 1992; Book & Eisenberg, 1979; Fuller, 1969; Staton-Spicer & Bassett, 1979; Williams, 1986), Figure 3.1 indicates that aspiring teachers typically move through a developmental sequence regard-

Senior Learner	Colleague-in-Training	Junior Colleague
Indicators of TA and RA Development		
Concerns		
Self/survival	Skills	Outcomes
TAs	TAs	TAs
How will students like me?	*How do I lecture, discuss?*	*Are students getting it?*
RAs *How will I fit on the research team? Will I be able to do the tasks expected of me?*	RAs *How should sampling be done to ensure a quality result? How can I report out the data most effectively?*	RAs *What is the significance of the findings?*
Discourse Level		
Presocialized	Socialized	Postsocialized
TAs and RAs	TAs and RAs	TAs and RAs
Give simplistic explanations	*Talk like insiders, use technical language*	*Make complex ideas clear without use of jargon*
Approach to Authority		
Dependent	Independent or Counterdependent	Interdependent/collegial
TAs and RAs	TAs and RAs	TAs and RAs
Rely on supervisor, supervisory committee	*Stand on own ideas— defiant at times*	*Relate to faculty as junior colleagues*
Approach to Students (TAs)		
Engaged/vulnerable, student as friend, victim or enemy	Detached/student as experimental subject	Engaged/professional student as client
"Love" students, want to be friends, expect admiration or are hurt, angry in response, personalize interactions	*Disengage or distance themselves from students—becoming analytical about learning relationships*	*Understand student/ instructor relationships and the collaborative effort required for student learning to occur*

Figure 3.1. Indicators of TA and RA Development

SOURCE: Adapted from Nyquist, Abbott, Wulff, and Sprague, *Preparing the Professoriate of Tomorrow to Teach: Selected Readings in TA Training.* Copyright © 1991 by Kendall/Hunt Publishing Company. Reprinted with permission.

ing the type of concerns they exhibit about their teaching. At first, beginning teachers are likely to express a preponderance of self concerns. They will wonder about what they should wear, whether students will like them, and whether they can fit the role of teacher at all. Following their survival concerns, beginning teachers then typically move to wonder about what methods they should be employing with students. Can I lecture effectively? Can I lead a class discussion? Can I maintain discipline? Will I be able to grade papers, construct tests? The last phase of aspiring teachers' concerns, after they feel somewhat competent in their interactions with students, is concern for impact on the student. Only then will they begin to wrestle with questions about how much students are learning or why students apparently cannot demonstrate on tests what they seem to understand in discussions or how they can get students more engaged in learning the material.

Research Assistants. Although the original conception of development (Sprague & Nyquist, 1991) included only TAs, we have been gratified to hear from many RAs and their supervisors that the framework fits them as well. They, too, begin with survival concerns. They wonder if they will be perceived as professionals, if they know enough, if they will be able to get along with their supervisors, if they will fit the role of a researcher at all. Following those concerns, RAs typically move to concerns about the tasks they are to perform. How should the sampling be done? Can they figure out the next steps in the experiment? How can they most effectively report out data to their supervisors and others? Only after that phase can RAs tend to the questions about the importance of the research and puzzle about questions surrounding the results, questions of ethics, and questions concerning the implications of the work.

Determining the level of concerns of teaching and RAs is not difficult. You can just ask them when they come together as a group, or you can assess the stages of development when you send your initial letter, as suggested in Chapter 2. Sample questionnaires for both TAs and RAs are included in Appendixes A and B of this chapter.

Asking TAs and RAs about their concerns actually assists in developing relationships with them whether at the senior learner, colleague-in-training, or junior colleague levels. The key to assisting

TAs and RAs is to accept their concerns as valid and tailor your response to the level they exhibit.

Beginning Teachers'/
Researchers' Talk

Teaching Assistants. A second dimension useful in assessing developmental stages of TAs has to do with how they talk about their discipline. At the novice level, sometimes called a presocialized level, the thinker in a particular discipline does not understand the complexities and ambiguities or conventions of a discipline. At this level, TAs are sometimes very successful in the classroom. Precisely because they talk like the students they teach, undergraduates seem to be able to understand them. At this novice level, however, we all know that complex ideas can be simplified beyond their usefulness. As graduate students become more immersed in their understanding of the discipline, they are really inducted into a community of scholars that uses precise technical vocabularies to explain the complexities and relationships of concepts. It is at this stage in their own development that TAs may not communicate effectively with undergraduate students. Needing a place to practice their new understandings and vocabulary where they will not be evaluated by mentors or peers, they often choose their students as audiences for trying out complicated explanations—sometimes even about narrowly focused research problems. Sometimes, they dismiss the elementary level that they now believe they must assume to explain material to undergraduates. Only when they move to the postsocialized phase will they be able to see that explaining difficult concepts in simple, clear ways is the mark of advanced intellectual development in a field of study. As Oliver Wendell Holmes reminded us so many years ago, "I do not give a fig for the simplicity that comes before complexity, but I would lay down my life for the simplicity that follows complexity."

Research Assistants. Graduate student researchers develop along similar lines in their discourse about their disciplines. Arriving in your department, your RAs are likely to be at different places along the continuum. They may have just completed their BA or BS, or they may have completed their MA or MS elsewhere and are now arriving to begin a Ph.D. program, or they may have a postdoctoral appointment, which should mean they are at the postsocialized stage. Listen to how they talk about their research and its place within the discipline. Do they speak simplistically about the research and the discipline, or are they practicing their newly acquired technical language, sometimes or often obfuscating meaning, or are they now at the point where they can use the clearest language available to explain their research efforts?

TAs and RAs must be taught that professional maturity requires the ability to translate and connect knowledge across disciplines and in clear ways to novice learners. Whether or not the graduate students make teaching a part of their future careers, they will always need to communicate their specialized knowledge to others outside their discipline, and they must be taught the value of such competence.

Beginning Teachers'/Researchers' Approaches to Authority

A third dimension for assessing the development of your TAs and RAs is their approach to authority. Once again, we believe that novice teachers and researchers go through definite stages. Usually, graduate students choose their graduate school based on reading the work of scholars at that institution or on the basis of the recommendations of their prior professors. Very enamored with the scholars with whom they have come to work, beginning graduate students depend heavily on their supervisors. You are held in high esteem, often emulated, and quite frequently quoted and imitated. As maturity comes, however, so does a time of dissociating from authority figures. To develop a sense of self and confidence in their own ability, graduate students must break away from supervisors to establish separateness and, eventually, independence. This period of counterdependency is sometimes very difficult for you as a graduate student supervisor. It is the people to whom you have been giving substantial amounts of time and energy who suddenly no longer seek or even adhere to your recommendations or advice. As a supervisor, you must identify this stage as a maturing one—a signal that the graduate student is outgrowing his or her dependence on you and moving to the final stage of professional development that is not autonomy at all, but rather is the joining of a community of professionals that will establish mature, collegial relationships where all viewpoints are prized and sought after. "Managing the ebbs and flows of professional connection, gracefully abandoning the flattery of a young scholar's hero-worship, taking differences of opinion seriously but not personally—these are some of the most challenging demands placed on senior colleagues who work with TAs [and/or RAs]" (Sprague & Nyquist, 1991, p. 308).

Beginning Teachers' Approaches to Students

Teaching Assistants. The final dimension, the TA's approach to students, may be more highly developed among the TAs than the RAs. As mentioned earlier, however, all professionals must teach others in some capacity, so all graduate students, TAs and RAs, must be able to establish effective teaching relationships with others. Their ability to do so reflects similar developmental changes that occur in graduate students' attitudes toward authority. Likewise, they think differently about students as they themselves develop. Beginning TAs are often likely to be very engaged with their students. The TAs will assess, almost on a daily basis, their feelings toward their students. Sometimes, they desire to become close friends with their students; they definitely want to feel needed by their students. Often becoming advocates for undergraduates who are experiencing what they feel to be unjust practices by faculty members, TAs may involve themselves very personally in the welfare of their students. Conversely, even with all their efforts, they may soon find that students miss class, fail to hand in homework, do not score as high on examinations as the TA was expecting, and thus are a source of disappointment and frustration. TAs may feel betrayed. At this stage, they will often advise new TAs that they "should not smile until after Thanksgiving" and that they should be on their guard at all times in their interactions with students. The students sometimes become the "enemy." Again, the actions of students become very intense and personalized in the mind of the TA, whether the actions are positive or negative.

Following this phase, TAs often withdraw from students to avoid being hurt or feeling vulnerable. They become quite detached and see students as much less exciting and/or much less demanding. The TA often becomes very legalistic during this phase, directing all student inquiries to the syllabus and developing numerical schemes to avoid the making of subjective judgments.

Finally, the TA develops a way of being very engaged with students while not taking all student behavior personally. To reach this stage, the TA will have developed skills for assessing students' needs and will treat them as highly valued clients, creating a relationship that benefits them both.

Research Assistants. We have experienced, and other supervisors of RAs have reported, similar developmental stages in research students, particularly when more experienced researchers mentor and teach novice RAs. Researchers and more experienced RAs sometimes hold expectations that are too high for the beginning researcher, forgetting their own behavior and competence at that stage. As a result, they may become frustrated and distance themselves from their apprentices. Finally, experienced researchers gain an understanding of the development of less experienced RAs and can relate to them in ways that not only challenge but also support the less experienced individual's growth and development.

Although not a perfect science, we believe that observing and listening to graduate students along the four dimensions of their concerns, discourse, attitudes toward authority, and attitudes toward students will enable you to determine approximately where your students are and assist you as you develop your own role in relation to the unique developing individuals that they are. *One size does not fit all,* and listening to their talk should alert you to their progress. Adjusting your supervisory relationships to meet their needs is the real challenge.

Supervisory Relationships
With TAs/RAs

Adapting your leadership to the maturity of the TAs and RAs is the next important step. Although discipline and department practices and conventions will no doubt dictate expectations that are the same for all TAs and RAs, you can make a difference. As we know, graduate students who are at the beginning stage of senior learner require closer supervision, considerable direction, and substantial personal support. As graduate students mature, they will require less directive assistance, but they will need you to model the behaviors and characteristics of a professional in the field. Finally, in the junior colleague stage, they will benefit from your treating them as young professionals by assuming the role of consultant and colleague. For this to happen, you need to practice progressive delegation, which will result in a gradual transfer of responsibility from you to them. A helpful way to think about accomplishing this progressive delegation can be illustrated in Figure 3.2.

As discussed earlier, your role will change as the TAs and RAs progress, and as indicated on Row 1 of the figure, we have labeled the primary roles you will assume as that of manager, educational model, and mentor. The assignments for TAs and RAs should also show a progression from that of specified duties under supervision to development of independence whether in teaching or research as reflected in Rows 2 and 3 of the figure. Teacher training activities for the TAs should follow this pattern also, moving again from close supervision to collegial sharing of ideas regarding curricular and pedagogical decisions. Finally, as is indicated in Row 5, your assessment practices also should reflect the progression of TAs and RAs as they assume more and more responsibility.

No matter where graduate students fit along the continuum from senior learner to colleague-in-training to junior colleague, they need to be provided adequate preparation for the roles you expect them to assume. Hopefully, you will assign roles appropriately, according to the TA's and researcher's development, in a continuous progression that will assist graduate students to develop as fully as possible. When we think about our roles as supervisors in these more complex ways, we begin to understand what it means to develop and oversee a meaningful apprenticeship, a challenge that demands our

	Senior Learner	Colleague-in-Training	Junior Colleague
Relative Emphasis on Supervisor's Role	Manager "Do the task my way and check back with me."	Educational Model "Think about the problem, generate options, and let's discuss potential outcomes."	Mentor "You make the decision. Let me know if I can be of help to you. I'm interested in the outcome."
Teaching Assignments for TAs	Assist professor Grade papers Hold office hours Conduct carefully planned quiz sections Collect feedback on course	Assume larger role in course Develop writing assignments Generate test questions Do some lecturing	Design and teach a basic course Assist with an advanced course
Research Assignments for RAs	Assist professor Perform specific duties under supervision	Assume design responsibility for part of grant or for own research project	Conduct research project using supervisor as a resource
Teacher Training Activity for TAs	Orientation Scheduled meetings Observation by supervisor Frequent feedback	Proseminar designed to build repertoire of teaching skills Observation and feedback from supervisor	Reflective practicum over curricular and pedagogical development and potential approaches to students
Function of Evaluation	Frequently assess performance in teaching and research assignments	Provide systematic feedback on the development of individual instructional and research skills	Provide feedback as a colleague on developing a personal teaching or research style and approach

Figure 3.2. Implications of the Three Phases of TA and RA Development for Supervision

SOURCE: Adapted from Sprague, J., & Nyquist, J. D. (1989). TA Supervision. In J. Nyquist, R. Abbott, & D. Wulff (Eds.), Teaching Assistant Training in the 1990's (p. 47). *New Directions for Teaching and Learning*, no. 39. San Francisco, Jossey-Bass.

best mental work. Adjusting your supervision as TAs/RAs develop will ensure a productive relationship that will contribute much to the emergence of competent professionals.

To provide such an experience for your TAs and RAs requires a very careful analysis of their development in relation to the responsibilities, whether in teaching or in research, that they are being asked to assume. In Chapter 4, we outline the special challenges in supervising graduate students who are serving as TAs; and in Chapters 5 and 6, we address the specifics of the roles of both graduate TAs and graduate RAs. Chapter 7 addresses the special challenges of international TAs (ITAs).

APPENDIX A

TA Questionnaire

This questionnaire is part of an effort to provide supervision that best meets your instructional interests and needs as you assume your TA appointment in the Department of XXXX. We hope that you will take this opportunity to tell us a little about your experience in the role of teacher: areas where you feel you have expertise and areas where you would like to expand and improve your teaching. If you have not taught before (as is true of many beginning TAs), please indicate that and identify areas that are of particular interest to you.

I. Previous Experience and Teaching Interests:

    A. Identify your teaching experience, if any:
        Courses you have taught (include level, title of course, and institution or organization)

    B. List your previous teaching roles:
        Sole instructor:
        Team teacher:
        TA with own section:
        Demonstrator:
        Grader or tutor:
        Other teaching experience:

    C. Please briefly describe any training programs on teaching methods or teaching effectiveness programs in which you have participated:

In our department you will most likely be involved in _____

(assisting a professor, holding office hours, tutoring, grading, leading field trips, conducting quiz/discussion sections and laboratories, teaching studio courses, or assuming full responsibility for a course as the instructor of record, etc.)

Please take a few moments to identify your level of experience and interest in each of the following aspects of teaching by circling the appropriate numbers:

(You, as a TA supervisor, need to select from the following list those items most appropriate to match the TA roles. You may need to augment the items to customize the questionnaire for your TAs.)

A. Holding office hours for students

| Little experience | 1 | 2 | 3 | 4 | 5 | Extensive experience |
| Little interest | 1 | 2 | 3 | 4 | 5 | Extensive interest |

B. Assisting in large enrollment classes

| Little experience | 1 | 2 | 3 | 4 | 5 | Extensive experience |
| Little interest | 1 | 2 | 3 | 4 | 5 | Extensive interest |

C. Working with students of diverse backgrounds

| Little experience | 1 | 2 | 3 | 4 | 5 | Extensive experience |
| Little interest | 1 | 2 | 3 | 4 | 5 | Extensive interest |

D. Conducting labs

| Little experience | 1 | 2 | 3 | 4 | 5 | Extensive experience |
| Little interest | 1 | 2 | 3 | 4 | 5 | Extensive interest |

E. Developing demonstrations for labs

| Little experience | 1 | 2 | 3 | 4 | 5 | Extensive experience |
| Little interest | 1 | 2 | 3 | 4 | 5 | Extensive interest |

F. Lecturing to large classes

| Little experience | 1 | 2 | 3 | 4 | 5 | Extensive experience |
| Little interest | 1 | 2 | 3 | 4 | 5 | Extensive interest |

G. Lecturing to small classes

| Little experience | 1 | 2 | 3 | 4 | 5 | Extensive experience |
| Little interest | 1 | 2 | 3 | 4 | 5 | Extensive interest |

H. Leading class discussions

| Little experience | 1 | 2 | 3 | 4 | 5 | Extensive experience |
| Little interest | 1 | 2 | 3 | 4 | 5 | Extensive interest |

I. Teaching studio classes

| Little experience | 1 | 2 | 3 | 4 | 5 | Extensive experience |
| Little interest | 1 | 2 | 3 | 4 | 5 | Extensive interest |

J. Conducting field work

| Little experience | 1 | 2 | 3 | 4 | 5 | Extensive experience |
| Little interest | 1 | 2 | 3 | 4 | 5 | Extensive interest |

K. Using technology in teaching (e-mail, multimedia, computing)

| Little experience | 1 | 2 | 3 | 4 | 5 | Extensive experience |
| Little interest | 1 | 2 | 3 | 4 | 5 | Extensive interest |

L. Developing writing assignments

| Little experience | 1 | 2 | 3 | 4 | 5 | Extensive experience |
| Little interest | 1 | 2 | 3 | 4 | 5 | Extensive interest |

M. Evaluating writing assignments

| Little experience | 1 | 2 | 3 | 4 | 5 | Extensive experience |
| Little interest | 1 | 2 | 3 | 4 | 5 | Extensive interest |

N. Developing multiple choice tests

| Little experience | 1 | 2 | 3 | 4 | 5 | Extensive experience |
| Little interest | 1 | 2 | 3 | 4 | 5 | Extensive interest |

O. Developing essay tests

| Little experience | 1 | 2 | 3 | 4 | 5 | Extensive experience |
| Little interest | 1 | 2 | 3 | 4 | 5 | Extensive interest |

P. Developing problem-solving tests

| Little experience | 1 | 2 | 3 | 4 | 5 | Extensive experience |
| Little interest | 1 | 2 | 3 | 4 | 5 | Extensive interest |

Q. Critiquing performances, art work

| Little experience | 1 | 2 | 3 | 4 | 5 | Extensive experience |
| Little interest | 1 | 2 | 3 | 4 | 5 | Extensive interest |

R. Assigning grades

| Little experience | 1 | 2 | 3 | 4 | 5 | Extensive experience |
| Little interest | 1 | 2 | 3 | 4 | 5 | Extensive interest |

S. Designing courses and constructing syllabi

| Little experience | 1 | 2 | 3 | 4 | 5 | Extensive experience |
| Little interest | 1 | 2 | 3 | 4 | 5 | Extensive interest |

II. Teaching Strengths and Concerns

A. What do you think are your teaching strengths?

B. What are your major concerns about teaching?

C. As you anticipate your appointment as a TA, what do you feel you most need during our TA orientation and ongoing training program?

APPENDIX B

RA Questionnaire

This questionnaire is part of an effort to provide supervision that best meets your research interests as you assume your RA appointment in the Department of XXXX. We hope that you will take this opportunity to tell us a little about your experience in the role of researcher: areas where you feel you have expertise and areas where you would like to expand and improve your research skills. If you have not been involved previously with formal research (as is true of many beginning RAs), please indicate that and identify areas of interest to you.

I. Background

A. Identify your research experience:
Projects you have worked on (include brief descriptions, names of supervisors, length of time on project, and your responsibilities)

B. List research and statistical methods courses you have taken

II. Project Assignments

In our department, you will be assigned to a professor who has a funded research project and will be able to support you. You will meet and talk with all professors during the first 6 weeks of Autumn Quarter. At that time, you will be given a form on which to identify your preferences. Choosing a research advisor may be the most important decision you will make during your graduate career, so take great care in making your selection. From experience, we know that selecting someone whose personality and working style are compatible with yours is essential. We will do everything possible to honor your first or second preference. Choose wisely, based on thorough investigation of the possible opportunities.

Although your choice need not be made until November, we have included a list of professors and available projects to help you begin thinking about your decisions and also to acquaint you with the wide range of research in the department.

Some students have a particular area of research in mind; others do not. But you must think also about the professor you will work with, the kind of project work available, and the size of the research group. You will receive the forms for identifying your preferences and a schedule of professor presentations about their research upon your arrival in the department. In the meantime, we'd like some additional information about you to inform our planning.

A. Given the attached list of research projects, which two or three are of the most interest to you? (This is preliminary information and not binding in any way.)

1.

2.

3.

B. If you had an "ideal placement" as an RA, what would it consist of?

SOURCE: Adapted from a questionnaire used by the Department of Chemical Engineering, University of Washington, Seattle, WA.

4

Preparing Graduate Teaching Assistants for Special Challenges in Teaching

At the university level, teaching often becomes confused with presenting. The use of large classes, particularly for lower-division courses, has contributed to the perception that an effective lecturer in terms of presentational style equals an effective instructor. As we who have taught know very well, this view is severely limited. Our teaching assistants (TAs) must understand the complexity of the teaching act. Effective instructors, as outlined in Chapter 5, must be competent in numerous roles:

- Leading discussions
- Conducting laboratories
- Holding office hours
- Evaluating and grading students' work, and so on

In addition to these roles, effective instructors must exhibit three other, even more complex competencies:

- They must represent the disciplines they teach.
- They must accommodate diverse students who demonstrate a variety of learning styles and differences in prior understanding of the content being studied.
- They must be able to learn from what they are doing, to become analytical and reflective about their teaching, to test incrementally and systematically their choices of content and their pedagogical approaches.

As a supervisor of TAs in today's academic setting, you must prepare TAs to handle these responsibilities, both while they are working under you and for the time when they will begin their postgraduate careers, especially those graduate students who are joining the professoriate.

Preparing TAs to
Represent Their Discipline

In institutions with graduate programs, it is the TA who most often introduces undergraduates to a discipline. Sometimes, the TA provides the student with his or her only experience with the discipline. Interaction with a TA may constitute the total impression that an undergraduate has about what a particular discipline values, investigates, and contributes to human understanding. TAs are often the ambassadors of our disciplines, and we too often ignore this fact. As Bondeson (1992) reminds us:

Simply put, we profess our discipline. We stand up and display an existential commitment to those disciplines; and, by our act of teaching them, we show that those disciplines are embodied in our own lives. Our commitment to our discipline is our way of saying to our students, as we profess, that it is worthy of their consideration and their time. . . . When we teach, we represent to our students the power and importance of our disciplines, the effects that they have had on our own lives, and the importance that they have for other human enterprises. At the moment we teach, we are the only connection between the rich tradition of our disciplines and the students before whom we stand. (p. 5)

Because your TAs are most often the "front line" or first instructors that undergraduates experience in your discipline, you must ask yourself whether the graduate students in your department, who daily interact with undergraduates, can do what Bondeson describes? Can they:

- Embody the discipline with their own lives?
- Place introductory courses within an entire curriculum, and within the discipline, so that they can help undergraduates understand that the course represents only one aspect of the study of XXXX?
- Explain the intellectual contribution of the discipline to the human enterprise?
- Identify the methodologies most useful in generating those intellectual contributions?
- Answer questions that undergraduates have about advanced study of the discipline, possible careers for which the discipline prepares a student, and other reasons for taking more courses in the discipline?

One possible way of approaching this challenge is to assist your graduate students directly to think about how they represent their discipline. Having your TAs fill out the form on the next page (Figure 4.1) and then leading a discussion among them can lead to rich responses and prepare them for this important task. The exercise works particularly well when graduate students are teaching sections of the same course.

Even if your TAs can place the contributions of a course within the discipline and the discipline within our larger knowledge of human understanding, can they then help undergraduates to share this understanding? Do they have a repertoire of methods and clear, simple language for doing so?

One way to ensure that they do is to allow them to practice on each other, rather than on their undergraduate students. Role-playing is a very positive and helpful way of building repertoire. The role-play on page 37 or a modification of it could be conducted with a group of TAs that shares the same responsibilities.

Representing Your Discipline

Discipline_____

Course _____

What are the basic building blocks of knowledge that you want undergraduates to master as a result of participating in this lab session, quiz section, discussion section, office hour, writing of papers, field trip, studio, or course? (The question depends obviously upon the responsibilities of the TAs.)

How will your students be able to identify the relationships between those basic concepts that you have identified?

Once mastered, will your undergraduate students recognize how those basic concepts fit into the larger study of your discipline? What will they need to understand in order to do that?

What understanding will allow your students to recognize the contributions of your discipline to human understanding?

How can such concepts be learned most effectively by undergraduates? What approaches/methods will you use?

Figure 4.1 Form for Disciplinary Exercise

Goal: To identify approaches you can use to represent the discipline to undergraduates.

1. Your challenge is to answer the questions, "What is X course about, how does it fit into the curriculum of discipline XXX, and how does discipline XXX fit with other disciplines? In addition, which methods are most typically used to study discipline XXX, which courses follow this particular one, and which possible careers follow from studying discipline XXX?"

2. Decide in your group how you will go about answering these questions for undergraduates. Develop a strategy upon which group members can agree.

3. Appoint a spokesperson who will role-play the group's strategies. You have 15 minutes to complete this phase of the activity.

Figure 4.2. Role-Play: Representing Our Discipline

ROLE-PLAY INSTRUCTIONS FOR SUPERVISOR

Divide the group into small groups of about four to five TAs. Pass out copies of the instructions for the exercise given in Figure 4.2. If you have a small number of TAs, they can work in pairs, or you can use the whole group to design a strategy. The TAs should have about 10 to 15 minutes to prepare, appoint a role player, and reconvene. At that time, you will instruct the large group to behave as undergraduate students, while each spokesperson in turn tries each group's plan. Because the members of each group will act as coaches, the spokesperson does not need to feel pressured to "get it right." If he or she becomes stuck, the group members can offer assistance. After each role-play, you can lead a discussion, asking such questions as:

- Did this approach help you to understand the course and its place within the discipline of XXX?
- Do you better understand the discipline of XXX and its contributions to the human enterprise?
- Was it clear to you what subsequent courses in the department would be appropriate for you to enroll in?

Even if they can competently answer questions about the discipline, do your TAs know when sharing such information is most appropriate? One guideline is that most undergraduates need to master elements of a particular course before they are apt to be interested in where that course fits into a curriculum and a field of study. We often observe TAs telling undergraduates on Day 1 all about the discipline and never talking with undergraduates about it again. Day 1 is when undergraduates are least likely to be able to assimilate such information. You can help your TAs by outlining with them an appropriate way to address such questions with undergraduates and the most effective time for providing such information.

Preparing TAs to
Accommodate Diverse Students

As we have written elsewhere (Nyquist, 1993; Wulff, 1993), graduate TAs, as all teachers in higher education, tend to teach as they have been taught. After at least 17 years of observing teaching, primarily modeled in ways that more recent research in cognitive processing is currently questioning, graduate students typically imitate what they have seen teachers and professors do that helped them to learn, and TAs often have difficulty in accommodating students who learn in other ways. There are reasons for this. First, all teachers, even novice ones, hold powerful visions of teaching based on their own learning experiences that permeate and dominate their teaching practices (Brookfield, 1990; Nyquist, 1993), and as Wulff (1993) observes, "Making changes in teaching entails identifying deeply-rooted assumptions in our own personal visions and that change may be not immediate" (p. 392). Second, TAs obviously have been successful in navigating the various minefields involved in learning and have risen to the top of those involved in academic settings. Otherwise, you would not be working with them. Although this provides intelligent, enthusiastic, committed graduate students, we must remember that they now may be among those least likely to understand students who do not share their preferred learning styles and their levels of commitment.

Research in teaching and learning has forced us to confront the student as a coconstructor of knowledge (Prawat, 1989; Resnick, 1989; Scardamalia & Bereiter, 1985). This view of learning has made us recognize that students individually must make sense out of what they are to learn, dealing with their own personal prior understandings as they attempt to assimilate the new information. TAs must learn to check continuously the level and accuracy of their students' understanding and modify their approaches to ensure that students are learning. "Telling" students is no longer sufficient, as if it ever was; rather, we must teach TAs that the outcome of instruction relies not on how organized and brilliant the lecture was but, instead, on the demonstrated understanding of the learner.

We have come to understand that there are various ways for students to learn, and that we must pay attention to the needs of nontraditional students, such as ethnic minorities (soon to be the majority in many institutions), returning adults, students with disabilities, women students, and those of a variety of sexual orientations. As Darling (1992) points out,

> The *fact of* diversity is more important than any particular *form of* diversity. In other words, it will not be possible or relevant to consider all the content of all the combinations of cultural clashes that might be experienced in an undergraduate classroom characterized by diversity. It *is* very possible and quite relevant, on the other hand, to examine the *fact of* culture clashes, how they happen in a classroom, and what implications exist for communicating in the classroom. . . . The *real* problems presented by diversity are attitudinal and not cognitive; thus, preparing TAs for student diversity will, of necessity, involve first attitudinal change and secondarily cognitive and behavioral change. (pp. 60, 61)

Darling goes on to suggest that TA supervisors must be prepared to talk about race. If you feel you need assistance in discussing issues such as race, stereotyping, marginalized students, and so on, you should contact your institution's unit that is directly involved in creating an inclusive environment. They usually provide speakers, workshops, and other activities tailored to your specific needs. The goal is to have "safe" discussions about diversity as it occurs in the classroom. You could also compile resource files of materials such as those listed in Chapter 10 for your TAs that will address the numerous ways in which diversity affects the educational environment. Hopefully, an outcome of such reading will be discussion groups or at least talk among the TAs about how to make assignments accessible to all members of the class. Rather than silencing alternative voices, TAs must learn how to conduct class sessions as active sessions of sharing knowledge in a cooperative way. More time must be spent on teaching TAs to lead such discussions than is currently spent on acquiring those skills.

Obviously, many of our colleagues and experienced faculty are finding it difficult to make adjustments, both to our new understanding of the learning process and to a student body that has changed dramatically over the past 25 years. Maybe you have been struggling with these issues. It is not easy to change from a homogeneous perspective about teaching to the new challenge, but you must assist your TAs to view teaching in this way in order for them to be effective with the undergraduates they are instructing currently and to hone their competencies for postgraduate careers inside and outside of the academy.

Teaching TAs to Be Analytical and Reflective About Their Teaching

Much has been written about being reflective about one's profession, particularly since Schön's book titled *Educating the Reflective Practitioner* was published in 1987. As he reminds us, not only can reflection help improve instruction, but it is professionally renewing.

> When a practitioner becomes a researcher into his own practice, he engages in a continuing process of self-education. When practice is a repetitive administration of techniques to the same kinds of problems, the practitioner may look to leisure as a source of relief, or to early retirement, but when he functions as a researcher-in-practice, the practice itself is a source of renewal. (p. 29)

Everyone seems to agree that being analytical and reflective about teaching is "good." Teaching people how to do this good thing, however, seems to be difficult.

What is ironic about this situation is that academicians are care-fully and thoroughly trained to be analytical and reflective in all their research efforts. Somehow, graduate students, and often pro-fessors, do not transfer those highly developed analytical skills to their teaching. Having been given no formal preparation for teach-ing, they treat the teaching act as a mystery, as behavior occurring without examination of the actions of instructor and students or the results of those actions.

As Fred Campbell, Dean of Undergraduate Education and Vice Provost at the University of Washington, is fond of saying, "Teach-ing may be the only human activity which a person can practice and practice and actually get worse at." We all know professors who, as years go by, do seem to deteriorate in their success as teachers. Often, those same professors are getting better and better at their research. Typically, we attribute that discrepancy to a matter of where professors spend their time in the age-old tension of teaching versus research. But we believe that there is an additional factor: the absence of a systematic way of analyzing and reflecting upon their teaching to gain insights to make changes to again reflect upon.

Chism's (1993) model (see Figure 4.3) is useful in representing the differences between a reflective practitioner and one who is not: As she displays, teachers who identify the problem and respond in systematic ways to collect data that will inform them are then able to reflect deeply and identify reasons for success or failure. Teachers who have no systematic way of analyzing their teaching tend to go on gut reaction and end up with little or no idea of what worked or did not work and why.

Reflecting on practice is really the key to making changes that will make TAs and all of us effective in our interactions with stu-dents. The constant "shooting from the hip" philosophy that all too often occurs in higher education when instructors have had no formal training in teaching is not conducive to discovering what works and what does not with sufficient evidence to make future curricular and pedagogical decisions. As reflected in Chism's model, the instructor who has not learned to be deeply reflective about his or her practice has little to go on when making future decisions about teaching. Hoping things will work or blaming instructional failures on students will not only create dissatisfaction but will also

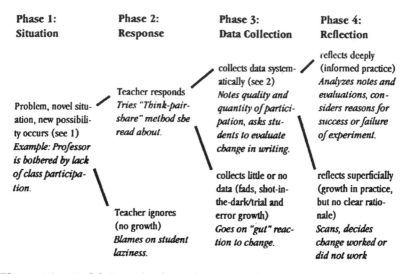

Figure 4.3. Model: Episode of Teaching Growth

SOURCE: Reprinted by permission of The National Center on Postsecondary Teaching, Learning, and Assessment. Copyright © 1993, NCTLA.

lead to instructor burnout. It is difficult to persist if one's efforts do not bring success.

As we work with TAs, we try to get them to apply the same tools that they use in their research to analyze and reflect upon their teaching. We even use a research perspective when we consult with them about what is going on in their classes, as is reflected in our consulting model represented in Figure 4.4.

Our model simply suggests that academicians can use the same tools in their teaching and research to arrive, systematically and incrementally, at new insights. In our research endeavors, attention is given to forming the research question, selecting the most appropriate method of collecting data that will provide useful information in answering the question, applying effective analytical procedures, and identifying implications of our results and connections to previously understood phenomena or extensions for further needed research. The same rigorous, logical steps can and should be applied to our teaching.

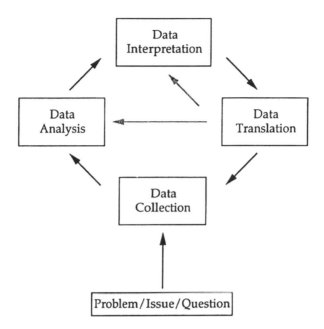

Figure 4.4. Consultation: A Research Process

Beginning with an *issue* or a *puzzling situation* raises questions. "Why did the students rate the TA as not organized when she believes she is very organized?" The next step is to *collect appropriate data*. The TA's self-report consists of very organized lecture notes and a syllabus that spells out her expectations for students. Because this evidence does not match that of the students, additional data are sought. Interviewing students or observing or videotaping are all processes that provide rich data for the instructor. In this case, the supervisor found that the TA was not using the board in an organized manner, leaving half-finished ideas that students wrote down as she hurried on to the next topic. Because of the TA's hurried approach and constant shuffling of notes, the supervisor could understand why the students felt she was disorganized. Interviewing students confirmed the supervisor's initial impression.

Interpreting the new data for the TA was the next step. After identifying the many strengths noted in the observation and in student comments, the supervisor defined what the students saw as disorganization—the key to understanding their evaluations. The final step was to determine how to *translate that information* into new approaches or instructor behaviors that the instructor could adopt. In this case, the TA learned to begin each class by outlining on the upper left-hand corner of the board the topics in the order that she would cover them during that class period. When viewing her videotape, the TA had been as amazed at how much information she talked about and held students accountable for but that did not appear on the board. She practiced completing what she wrote on the board or the overhead projector by asking a student to share her notes with her each day. The subsequent ratings by students showed great progress. Her students saw her as very organized. Why test scores were lower than the TA expected (a new issue) became the next question that the TA attacked—cycling through the model as she had done in the case of her difficulties with organization. Thus, she became systematic in her attempts to become a more effective instructor. Her efforts paid off and resulted in greater student satisfaction and improved student performance.

There are many other approaches to assisting TAs to become reflective and systematically more effective in their teaching. Angelo and Cross (1993) provide numerous ways of assessing student understanding and satisfaction with their learning. A most important challenge for you, as a TA supervisor, is to provide your TAs processes by which they can reflect upon their teaching so that as they leave your department and your supervision, they become thoughtful assessors of their own teaching competence. Successful teaching requires that we be lifelong learners, committed to understanding how we can most skillfully engage our students' minds in meaningful intellectual exchange. Learning that lesson early—at the graduate level—will greatly enhance the professional growth of a teacher/scholar in higher education.

Thus, the special challenges of representing the discipline, accommodating diversity, and becoming reflective about teaching must become part of your work with TAs. We have suggested only a few ways of covering these important topics, but hope our ideas will stimulate you to reflect upon how that work might be accomplished with your particular group of TAs. In addition to these special challenges, graduate TAs must master specific teaching competencies, which we outline in the next chapter.

5

Preparing Graduate Teaching Assistants for Their Specific Instructional Roles

An important step in working with teaching assistants (TAs) is to identify and understand the specific instructional roles they will fulfill. Clearly, those roles will vary in different departments and on different campuses. We have used this chapter to (a) clarify the information and skills that TAs need in their major roles and (b) identify some of the particular challenges and suggest strategies that you can use in working with TAs. The roles discussed in the chapter include:

- Assisting the professor
- Holding office hours/tutoring
- Leading field trips
- Conducting quiz/discussion sections
- Conducting laboratories
- Teaching studio courses
- Assuming full responsibility for a course as the "instructor of record"
- Evaluating and grading

Because some TAs have multiple roles, we have included in Figure 5.1 a matrix that can assist you in thinking about the needs of your TAs. After listing your TAs' names in the left column, make a check by each role your TAs will be asked to assume. This will provide you with an inventory of the roles for which you will need to prepare them.

Assisting the Professor With a Course

When the job is to assist the professor, the responsibilities for TAs vary widely because they are determined by the individual faculty member. Those duties might include being involved with the design of the course; assisting in identifying and collecting resource material; constructing tests; helping with daily logistics, such as preparation, materials, and equipment; grading assignments or papers; answering student questions before and after class; or meeting individually with students. Occasionally, TAs in these roles might assume responsibility for teaching a class or leading group activities. The following guidelines can help you prepare TAs for assisting with a course in various ways.

Strive to Minimize Ambiguity. More than other roles in which the TA leads a section or lab or grades papers, the role of assisting the professor has great potential for ambiguity.

- Thus, it is imperative that you provide TAs who assist you with clear instructions about what you would like them to do. TAs report that they are uncomfortable when they feel they are supposed to be doing something but do not know what that something is. An important part of the supervisory process for TAs assisting you with a course is showing them how their roles fit into the larger picture of the course.
- You can help by discussing with them your goals for the course and what they might do to help you achieve the goals. Sometimes just reinforcing that having them in class to provide a listener's perspective is a way of helping you in the course.

Take Advantage of TA Expertise. You can learn much from the experiences of TAs, and they can benefit from having their expertise

TA	Assisting the Professor	Holding Office Hours/Tutoring	Leading Field Trips	Conducting Quiz/ Discussion Sections	Conducting Labs	Teaching Studio Courses	Assuming Full Responsibility for a Course	Evaluating, Critiquing, and Grading
1.								
2.								
3.								
4.								
5.								
6.								
7.								
8.								
9.								
10.								

Figure 5.1. Skills Needed by TAs

recognized and incorporated into your course. We recently talked to Marilyn and David, TAs who had returned to the university to obtain their PhDs after years of experience in other settings. David had been a counselor who supervised other counselors in elementary schools in a large school system. Marilyn had spent 11 years teaching mathematics in secondary schools. Both came to us looking for jobs that were more suitable to their levels of experience. As assistants to professors in their departments, their primary responsibilities were to photocopy, help make overhead transparencies, and record grades. Both Marilyn and David reported feeling so demeaned and unappreciated that they were ready to drop out of graduate school. As their stories suggest, when TAs have the knowledge and ability to teach lessons or interact with students, it is important that you find ways for them to do so, not only for their own development but also for the good of undergraduates who could benefit from their contributions.

Use Opportunities for Feedback. Many times, we have heard about how TAs want more feedback from their supervising instructors. Providing regular feedback for the TAs that assist you can serve two important functions:

- It can, of course, provide insights that will help the TAs in their development.
- In addition, though, the feedback helps you to clarify your needs and monitor whether you are using the TAs in the best way to assist both in the course and in their professional development.

Also, you can use the TA's role as an opportunity to obtain feedback about your course. Recently, a professor asked us to provide a midterm evaluation process that requires that we interview her undergraduate students about what was working well in helping them learn in the course and what could be changed to assist them in learning. Once we had prepared a summary of the information for the instructor, we prepared to meet with her to discuss the student feedback and help her decide how to respond to the student input. When she arrived for the discussion, the professor had brought with her the TA who was assisting her with the course. Her rationale was that the TA could provide another set of useful perceptions, particularly because in some ways, she is closer to the student perspective. During the discussion of the student perceptions, the faculty member encouraged the TA to express her perceptions of the course, to help explain the student perceptions, and, especially, to suggest specific ways that the professor might respond to the student input and enhance student learning in the course. As a result of this collaboration, the instructor received additional valuable insights about both what was happening in the course and what she could do to improve it. The TA learned a valuable lesson in the use of feedback for instructional improvement and went away confirmed by the instructor's confidence in her knowledge and experience.

Holding Office Hours/Tutoring

Sometimes TAs are responsible for working one on one or in small groups with students during office hours or in tutoring roles. Tutoring or holding office hours may be the only major assignment that a TA has, or it may be part of a larger assignment in a course, section, or laboratory in which a TA has another teaching assignment but is expected to provide additional one-on-one assistance for students. You can use the following ideas to help TAs make the time valuable for both themselves and the undergraduate students.

Emphasize That Holding Office Hours Is an Important Assignment. When TAs whose primary responsibility is to tutor or hold office hours compare themselves to TAs with responsibility to conduct a section, lab, or course, they sometimes end up short-changing the office hour/tutoring role by suggesting that "I *just* hold office hours" or "I am *only* a tutor." So, it is important to stress that working one on one with students is a teaching role, and, in some ways, it is teaching at its best because it provides the opportunity for the TAs to meet the specific needs of individual students. In addition, it provides the TAs with an opportunity to work with the students in a less formal, more interpersonal setting. Students express their approval when an instructor or TA offers additional instructional assistance beyond the class meeting time. On the other hand, if an instructor or TA misses a regularly scheduled office hour, word spreads quickly and students do not hesitate to point out that the instructor is not available as promised. The office hours are important also because they collectively provide TAs with insights into the kinds of ongoing questions and difficulties that students are having with course content and suggest areas for further review or instruction in the course.

Explain That Students Will Need Encouragement to Use Office Hours or Tutoring Services. Ironically, even though students expect instructors to be available during office hours or scheduled tutoring times, many students rarely use such services. You can assist the TAs to encourage students to use the potential of office hours by helping them think about the scheduling of office/tutoring hours. One TA we knew was doing everything that he perceived possible to accommodate students' needs in office hours but was having little success in getting students to use the office hour times. When we had the opportunity to talk to the students, they expressed their concern about the times the office hours were scheduled. The office hours were on Monday and Wednesday mornings. Students frequently got quizzes back on Wednesday afternoons and felt the need to discuss their grades and answers on the quizzes immediately. They reported, however, that by the next Monday morning, because they were well into preparing for the next weekly quiz, it was too late to go back and think about the previous quiz. As this example demonstrates, it is important to anticipate student needs when scheduling office/tutoring hours. On many occasions, students have expressed preference for office/tutoring sessions that are held immediately after the class with which the tutoring/office hours are associated. Also, TAs need to be willing to meet by special arrangement if students are unable to adapt their schedules to the regular times.

Because of the potential value of the office hours/tutoring, you also might suggest that the TAs:

- Require students (in smaller classes, of course) to attend one office hour before the first major assignment.

- Allow students with similar questions/concerns to come to office hours in small groups.
- Describe exactly what will happen when students show up for office hours or tutoring sessions so that the ambiguity and fear of the unexpected can be reduced for students who are timid.
- Provide office phone numbers or use e-mail with their students.

With any of the strategies, it is important that TAs send messages of genuine willingness to assist students. Undergraduate students do distinguish between "availability" and "approachability." They have told us that a person's "availability" during tutoring/office hours does not necessarily mean that they see him or her as "approachable." They are far more likely to "approach" someone whom they perceive as willing to assist—empathic, patient, and interested in their learning.

Point Out That Office Hour Instruction/Tutoring Requires Careful Listening. Listening is particularly important during tutoring or office hours because the success of such sessions is heavily dependent on careful assessment facilitated by listening. Initially, TAs will need to ask questions and listen carefully to determine where the students' needs lie and what students are lacking in terms of information and/or skills. Through this kind of listening, the TAs can meet needs much more quickly and readily. In addition, the approach sends strong messages about respect and desire to hear how students talk about what they are learning. Once the need is identified, good tutoring is still more than a process of explaining, giving examples or answers, or telling students what to do. Rather, TAs need to learn to ask students to talk out loud about how they are thinking about the information and/or skill and using it. This approach provides an opportunity for the TAs to provide ongoing assessment and guidance. As a final step in the one-on-one meeting, it is important for TAs to learn some informal techniques to assess whether the student has learned. Too often during such one-on-one sessions, students stare blankly and nod their heads in agreement but do not understand what they have heard and do not want to face the embarrassment of admitting that they did not understand. Thus, the TA might ask the student to talk through the concept discussed, give a different example, or work through a similar kind of problem—any approach with which the TA can assess the student's understanding of what has just been learned.

Encourage TAs to Use Frameworks to Organize Their Time With Students During Tutoring or Office Hours. Clearly, TAs cannot anticipate the many problems and issues that students might bring, and, in some ways, it is presumptuous to think they can plan for such a spontaneous event. Nevertheless, there are specific ways to think about various kinds of content, and preparing with frameworks in advance not only will help TAs prepare students to think about the content but will also help them realize that they can be prepared and confident for office hours or tutoring interactions. Some of the frameworks might be derived from your own discipline's way of thinking or from your own ways of thinking about your work. For instance, you might suggest a framework with five basic steps:

- Establishing rapport
- Diagnosing the need (concern, information, problem)
- Identifying a goal to be accomplished in the session
- Assisting the student in addressing the need
- Assessing whether the student understood

Although the rapport and final assessment will exist regardless of the kind of course and content, the kind of framework TAs use in the middle steps to get students to think about a problem or concern will depend on the content and the kinds of questions that students have.

Sometimes, a framework for solving mathematical problems will be helpful. We know TAs who help students think through problems during office hours by asking: First, "What is the problem asking you to do?" Then, "What information do you have and what information do you need to solve the problem?" Next, "Where can you find the needed information?" And, "How would you proceed then in using the information to solve the problem?" Finally, "How could you check to see if you have solved the problem correctly?" Similarly, in reviewing concepts, TAs might use a series of questions that checks to see, first, if students can define a concept ("So, how does the author define *contingent leadership*?"); if students understand the concept ("How would you explain *contingent leadership* in your own words?"), and then, perhaps, to provide an example ("Can you give me an example of *contingent leadership* in a business setting?").

Leading Field Trips

In a variety of courses, TAs may have responsibility for taking students on field trips. Students are partial to this instructional method, often viewing such outings as a break in the monotony that they perceive they experience with more traditional instructional methods. Instructors, although realizing that such outings can provide invaluable learning experience, also recognize that such an instructional method requires substantial time and effort in setting up logistics and coordinating specific activities to achieve the goals of a course. The challenge for TAs is to capture and retain the excitement of the instructional method for students while simultaneously making field trips a safe, efficient, and valuable learning experience. You can assist TAs in this role by addressing the following ideas.

Provide Background That Will Inform TAs About the Areas Visited. One of the challenges of having TAs take undergraduates on field trips is that even though the TAs may have developed expertise in the specific content area, because they come from different geographical locations and sometimes from different countries, they may not know a particular area well enough to explain it to students. Therefore, as a precursor to assigning TAs to the role of field trip leaders, you will have to inform them about the local resources available to them and their students. In geology, for example, you may have to go with the TAs and show them specific geological locations so that they feel more comfortable. In architecture, you may have to accompany the TAs on an initial trip in which you help them place a building in the historical context of the community. Such approaches provide ways for the TAs to know what it is like to experience an area for the first time and be closer to the experience when they share it with undergraduate students.

Point Out the Need to Achieve Balance Between Telling and Leading to Discovery. It works well to have the goals clearly identified before the field trip, and, unless there is a desire for discovery learning, to explain those goals explicitly to the students at the beginning of each field trip. Once the goals have been identified, the TAs can use them to plan what the students will do during the trip. In some cases, time constraints and lack of student background will necessitate the TAs' showing, pointing out, or simply telling the students about special features they are observing or specific steps they should take to develop the skills or acquire the content. These are the cases in which TAs should determine beforehand what skills or information they wish to emphasize. In other instances, however, TAs may want students to make their own discoveries. In these instances, the TAs should prepare questions that they can use to help students uncover the desired information or skills.

Questions can be particularly useful for keeping students focused and directly involved in what they are experiencing. For instance, if the TA wants architecture students to recognize the influence of the industrial revolution on particular buildings, the TA might, depending on the background of the students, begin with general questions, such as "What kinds of influences do you think shaped the architecture of this building?" If students do not have the background, the TA might take a few minutes to provide some background and review ideas that the students discussed in the course and then ask a more direct question such as, "So where do we see influences of the Victorian era as we look around this building?" Similarly, if forestry students are visiting a site for new forest growth, a general question might be, "What do you notice about the growth of vegetation as you look at this site?" More specific questions in which students apply previously learned information might be, "What kinds of trees are these? How old would you think they are?"

The point is that although students will occasionally have to be given background information or explanations, TAs should use questions to help students generate their own conclusions, which will keep them involved in the experience of the field trip. As supervisor, you can assist TAs in planning questions and in thinking about the appropriate balance between giving information and asking questions.

Stress the Safety of Students. It is important to emphasize for TAs the importance of safety and their responsibility as authority figures. Because students often are rightfully viewed as adults by TAs, safety is not considered an issue. However, with logistics of getting to and from the sites and variation in background and motivations of students, it is important for TAs to know the policies regarding safety in the same way that lab instructors need to be aware of and follow safety procedures. Without reducing the excitement and fun of the experiential learning process, TAs should be able to show that they are in charge and that they will take control if students behave in ways that endanger others or detract from the learning of the group. One way to assist less experienced TAs with their responsibilities as authority figures is for you and the more experienced TAs to identify the most common troublesome situations that new TAs are likely to encounter on field trips and to discuss those in groups so that the new TAs have a variety of ideas from which they can choose and with which they feel comfortable. Another possibility is to travel to the sites to conduct "dry runs" with the new TAs playing the roles of undergraduate students.

Require That TAs Maintain Records. One way to decrease your work in preparing TAs for field trips is to have TAs document their field trip experiences—logistics, impressions, highlights, and difficulties. Then, both you and the experienced TAs can subsequently use that information in preparing other new TAs.

Conducting Discussion Sections

As discussion section leaders, TAs identify the most important content from the lectures in the large class or from their syllabi or readings, set goals, and design lessons that elaborate on the information and expand students' understanding of it. In some instances, TAs also may be responsible for explaining and grading assignments based on the course activities in either the larger class or the section. We offer the following basic guidelines as you assist the TAs in their roles as leaders of discussion sections. Because student involvement is central to the role, we have focused the ideas on the interactive element of such sections.

Emphasize the Importance of Linking Discussion to Specific Goals. It is sometimes news to beginning instructors that facilitation of good class interaction requires careful preplanning. Particularly if they have had experience as students in classes with experienced facilitators of interaction, they may not realize that the facilitators spent as much time planning goals and questions as actually facilitating the in-class interaction. Therefore, as part of your supervisory role, you can assist TAs to recognize the importance of thinking specifically about the use of goals and questions in the process.

If TAs want to have students develop definitions, apply concepts, break ideas into parts, synthesize important ideas from several different sources, solve problems, or evaluate information, they need to identify those specific goals so that they know in which direction a discussion should go and how they want to move students in the appropriate direction. Discussion works better for some goals than others. For instance, it is clearly not the best way to impart information quickly and efficiently. Nor is it the best way for students to memorize formulas, definitions, or basic concepts. It is a useful strategy, however, when TAs want students to brainstorm, expand their thinking about a topic, or engage in interaction that enhances their skills. It is a particularly useful method when instructors want to hear students thinking aloud as they develop their ideas/skills. When retention of ideas is an important goal, class discussion is a particularly useful method because research suggests that students retain information longer if they say it or if they hear peers say it. Once TAs recognize the significance of planning goals for discussion, you can begin to help them understand how to involve students in the discussion process.

Undergraduate Students Need to Be Motivated to Participate in Discussion. Undergraduates have reported to us that they cannot get motivated to participate when the instructor begins with general, unstructured questions, such as "What are your questions about the large class lecture (or on your reading)?" or "What difficulties did you have with the problems assigned for this week?" Students often are reluctant to participate in a session that starts by showing what they do not understand. Furthermore, sometimes there is so much information that they heard, read, or tried to apply that they do not even, as they put it, "know what it is that we don't know." Therefore, you might suggest ways that TAs can motivate students to participate:

- Use brief narrative accounts of personal experiences to set the context for good classroom interaction. For instance, if TAs wanted a discussion to focus on health services, they might start the class by telling a personal account of a recent accident in which they were injured. Or, they might ask students to cite examples that they felt comfortable sharing about their own experience with health care. Then, TAs could pull out pieces of the examples that lead into the issues and information that they want to use in the discussion. In an economics section, the TA might talk about the first time he understood the concept of opportunity cost, or what he gave up in order to do what he had chosen to do.
- Administer a brief, short-answer, oral or written quiz (probably just for practice) that students can complete individually or in groups. The quiz can then provide the impetus for students' understanding of what is important to know and what they might need to review in order to learn the material.
- Provide a brief case that illustrates major concepts, or ask one or two overriding questions—some kind of stimulus that students can work on in small groups (three to five students) before the class interaction. The information from the smaller group can then provide the basis for the larger class discussion.

The point in these suggestions is that you can assist TAs by helping them realize that the motivational step must precede efforts to facilitate students' participation.

Help TAs Learn to Wait for Student Responses to Questions. Chet Meyers (1986) has reinforced the importance of creative silence in contributing to students' development of critical thinking. Especially for inexperienced instructors, an issue in leading the interactive classroom is the wait time for student responses.

Students need time to catch up, to formulate responses, and even to talk through their ideas aloud when the TAs ask questions. However, because less experienced instructors are often uncomfortable with the ensuing silence or because they are in a hurry to cover the assigned content, they hasten to move on without giving students an opportunity to respond sufficiently. We recently observed a TA who unconsciously established rules about some students in his class raising their hands to respond and waiting to be called on, whereas others just jumped in to talk when they felt like it. When we asked him about these differences, he reported that he was not aware of the fact that some were raising their hands to be called on and others were not. The next time we observed, we tried to determine what dynamics might be operating in the interaction in his classroom. Ultimately, through our ongoing discussions, we discovered that students who could respond quickly and move the discussion forward in directions that he perceived helpful were permitted to jump in and talk. Students who needed extended time to think, responded more slowly, and required help and additional probing questions to clarify their thinking were raising their hands, waiting patiently, and being called on less frequently.

As this example demonstrates, TAs may not even be aware of the dynamics that silence can create in their sections. You can assist by discussing the importance of silence and giving them opportunities to practice using it when they are asking and responding to student questions. The use of videotape critiques of classroom interaction, as discussed in the observation section of Chapter 8, is one way to help TAs recognize how they use wait time in their sections.

Conducting Laboratories

Through laboratories, TAs provide an opportunity for students to be more directly involved in demonstrations, experiments, and writing activities designed to facilitate their understanding of the content. Like the field trip, the laboratory is often an extension of a larger class. Typically, TAs who conduct laboratories are responsible for reviewing experiments beforehand, setting up laboratory materials, getting students started on their laboratory work, answering and asking questions to guide students, and evaluating students' progress. In such teaching roles, particularly in the sciences, TAs also must demonstrate knowledge about safety procedures and departmental/institutional policies regarding equipment in order to provide a safe environment in which students can work.

Use a Printed Document to Assist TAs With Their Laboratory Responsibilities. Because there are so many different issues and responsibilities related to conducting labs, TAs will find it useful if you can provide information in written form. On our campus, a Lead TA and two faculty members interviewed TAs and developed a brief document to respond to issues and concerns that TAs identified as important to them in the preparation for their laboratory roles (Samberg, Wiegand, & Selfe, 1993). When you develop such a document, it is important to get a sense of the needs of the TAs and then prepare a document that addresses those needs. Among the essential areas that you might address in such a document are responsibilities, teaching strategies, procedures for equipment and safety, assessment, and resources in the laboratory.

Stress the Importance of Advanced Preparation for Laboratory Activities. When asked what advice they would give incoming TAs about teaching labs, experienced TAs emphasize being prepared in advance for specific laboratory experiments or assignments. Similarly, when chemistry TAs who teach labs were asked to describe a situation in which things were going well in their laboratories, many suggested "that they were better teachers during their second section teaching the same experiment. Some also believed they performed better when they had done the laboratory experiment on their own before the students attempted it" (Samberg et al., 1993, p. 233). Thus, you can assist TAs by providing ways for them to prepare their laboratories in advance.

Suggest Ways to Prepare Undergraduate Students for Laboratory Work. Laboratory TAs do their best jobs of teaching if they can address potential difficulties in the laboratory before they arise. Because safety is an issue in many laboratories, for instance, you and other experienced TAs can assist less experienced TAs by telling them how you prepare students for safety procedures that will be enforced. If students work in laboratory pairs or small groups, you can assist the TAs in thinking about how, during the initial meeting of the laboratory, they can prepare students for working with a laboratory partner. Finally, you can give the TAs ideas about how to prepare students for each activity in the laboratory. Although students generally appreciate the "hands-on" learning in the laboratory, they have a strong need for clear expectations and, as they put it, "step-by-step instructions." In addition, undergraduates express the need for TAs to explain in clear, understandable language what has to be done for the exercise and what the write-up, if there is one, needs to look like. You can help TAs realize that because of their experience and preparation with a specific experiment, they can easily leave out important steps or connections between steps.

Make Suggestions About Interacting With Students in the Laboratory. Undergraduate laboratory students frequently cite accessibility as critical to good TA-student interaction in laboratories. The accessibility comes when the TA moves away from the front of the laboratory to circulate through the various stations, ask questions, and check students' understanding of what they are doing. It is strengthened by the TA's willingness to answer all questions with patience and concern for the students' learning. Because students expect such helpfulness, however, it is important to caution TAs about simply answering questions for the students or telling them next steps without first probing their understanding and asking questions that will help the students to come to their own conclusions and understandings.

Teaching Studio Courses

In some cases, TAs will assume the role of instructors or facilitators for studio courses in disciplines such as architecture, art, dance, or music. Studio courses present particular challenges for TAs because, more than some of the other roles, they involve the element of creativity. Unlike some of the roles in which TAs can identify specific goals and know in advance where they want students to be at the end, studios require the ability to probe, create, motivate, and move students in a creative direction where the end product, while achieving the goal of the assignment, is sometimes not so clearly defined. Some of the skills required of studio TAs, then, are different from skills required for the other roles. You can help TAs with studio responsibilities in some of the following ways.

Help TAs Recognize the Importance of Students' Prior Understandings. Undergraduates often come to their classes with preconceived notions about what can be accomplished and how their work will be evaluated. Although students' prior understandings are a factor in any teaching, they are especially relevant in studio classes. In some cases, the students may have had experiences with high school courses where creativity was encouraged above all else, and they received high grades simply for creating without the application of specific standards. In other cases, students, because of their developmental level, may believe that there are right and wrong answers and may strive in their work for some ideal that they think the instructor holds in his or her head.

For these reasons, it is important for TAs to think in advance about how they identify expectations for studio projects and how they relay those expectations to students. If a project is intended to push the creative boundaries of the students' abilities, TAs should be prepared to listen for such questions and comments as, "Is this the right way to do this?" or "I can't seem to get this color right." Such uses of the words *right* and *wrong* may indicate that the students are at a level where they are still expecting there to be an answer, or at least a right way to do the project. TAs will then have to think seriously about how to move students in their thinking to the idea that there may be several different ways that they could fulfill the requirements of the project.

Encourage the TAs to Set High Expectations for Students. Although high expectations should naturally accompany all of the instructional roles for TAs, inexperienced instructors, because of the element of creativity in studio classes, sometimes try to provide encouragement and support at the expense of high expectations. Yet in our work in a studio class, students expressed appreciation that the professor "expected high-quality work." They specifically appreciated the fact that she urged students to be observant in examining the world around them and to practice drawing what they saw.

Students also felt motivated by the fact that "Dr. Stanley pushes us to take risks and try new things, with color, for instance."

Help TAs Think About How to Provide Critiques. Although studio courses may, at times, require that TAs address the entire class or groups of students, TAs spend much of the time providing critiques. You can assist TAs by pointing out the following:

- Students appreciate having a number of critiques.
- They appreciate it when TAs listen during the critique process and avoid imposing their ideas too quickly.
- Because studio classes involve the close link between the artist and his or her work, a key is knowing when students do not have the necessary information and when to use questions to push students to apply what they already know.
- It is helpful when TAs are supportive but constructive in suggesting next steps or issues to consider as a design or project progresses.
- Students report that they benefit from solving their own problems after the difficulties have been pointed out.

Prepare TAs With the Necessary Visual Tools. Many studio instructors emphasize the importance of helping students visualize in studio courses. Students, too, stress the importance of "lots of examples and illustrations with slides, videotapes, and the computer." Thus, it is important that you help TAs think about how to incorporate a variety of visual examples in their work with either individual students or the entire class. Stress that TAs need to be aware of the resources in the department and the campus and then provide ways for them to determine what the most useful resources are.

Assuming Full Responsibility as "Instructor of Record"

Typically, full TA responsibility for a course comes when there are several sections of an introductory course (e.g., French). In some instances, though, TAs assume these roles when they reach a junior colleague stage and teach specialty courses. In these roles, TAs make many of the decisions about the course, under your indirect supervision, primarily outside the classroom. Thus, it is particularly important that you prepare TAs for this responsibility. All of the ideas about various roles in this chapter are relevant for TAs who are instructors of record. In addition, you will want to address the following suggestions.

Provide TAs With an Understanding of Basic Instructional Design. Although knowing how to design activities or classes for sections is an important part of the responsibilities for most TAs, such knowledge is particularly important for TAs who are responsible for their own courses. Too often, TAs report that they have no framework for thinking about how to design a course or a class period. They just jump in. They may start by making up assignments or thinking about asking questions or lecturing, often with little or no follow-up to see if material really has been learned. You can assist TAs by discussing with them a basic instructional framework that they can use in any teaching situation.

You can think about teaching as a process in four parts:

- Some way of determining needs
- Goals based on those needs
- Methods for achieving those goals
- Ways of determining whether the goals have been achieved

With this framework, TAs can be taught to think about each of these factors as a way of organizing a course, a specific lesson, or a particular session with a student. For example, TAs might think about who their students are, set goals to achieve with those students, determine about how best to achieve the goals with the particular students, and finally follow through to be sure the students understand. You can assist TAs by providing ample opportunities for them to talk to you, other faculty, experienced TAs, and other new TAs about all of the areas of such an instructional framework.

Help TAs Create a Syllabus. Once you have provided a framework and helped TAs think about design issues for their courses, your task is to help them capture that information in a syllabus. Although the design of syllabi may vary from department to department, it is important to view the syllabus as a contract between the instructor and the students. TAs should recognize the importance of the syllabus for explaining the problem, issue, or context that will be addressed through the content in the course; major goals to be achieved; an outline for addressing the content; guidelines for grading in the course; and any relevant information about expectations for student participation in the course. Stress to TAs that the syllabus can serve as a way to prevent difficulties later in the term related to mismatches between the expectations of the TAs and their students. Provide lots of sample syllabi as models and give TAs opportunities to ask questions of you, experienced TAs, and other faculty.

Prepare TAs for the First Days of Class. Time and time again in our work with TAs, we have heard the refrain, "If I had only known, I would have told the students on the first day of class how I intended to grade their participation (or that the final could not be taken early)." For concerns from the relatively harmless (a student reading a newspaper in class) to the severe (a student making a racist comment about another during a class discussion), TAs can be prepared with some advanced support from you. The key is to identify the kinds of situations that arise throughout the typical basic course in your discipline; have other faculty and experienced TAs assist you in identifying such situations. Then help the less experienced TAs develop specific strategies for addressing these issues as part of the expectations in the first days of the course.

Evaluating and Grading Student Work

In some cases, TAs will have responsibility as graders of student work. Although grading may be a primary responsibility of the TA role, it often is combined with other roles that TAs assume. Any time TAs assume the grading role, it is important for them and for you, as supervisor, to realize the importance of the role in the eyes of the students. Because undergraduates often perceive grades in terms of fairness, the way they are graded is the part of the instructional process that has the greatest potential for creating tension in the TA-student relationship. For specific suggestions in this area, you can refer to *Tips for Improving Testing and Grading* (Ory & Ryan, 1993). You can also diminish potential difficulties by addressing the following basic guidelines.

Reinforce for TAs the Link Between Goals and Grading Criteria. Although it seems apparent, not all beginning instructors recognize the importance of the relationship between goals and criteria for evaluation. When TAs grade student work, they need to know which goals have been targeted and which criteria are to be used to determine whether those goals have been accomplished. If TAs are establishing criteria as part of a section, lab, or course for which they have a major instructional responsibility that includes grading, it is important that they know how to set goals and establish grading criteria. Particularly when grading is subjective, for instance, when TAs are evaluating papers or essay exams, it is important that they develop the criteria in advance and find a way to make those criteria explicit when the assignment is presented to the students.

Be Sure TAs Know About All Relevant Grading Procedures and Policies. For TAs to do their best jobs in their roles as graders, it is important that they be aware of supervisor, departmental, and university procedures and policies that affect their grading of student work. For instance, we know that students appreciate getting their work graded and returned quickly. In addition, such a practice sends signals of respect to the students. If you wish to address an issue such as prompt return of assignments, and it is not already part of departmental or university policy, you can state it directly or provide it in written form as a guideline or policy to which you want TAs to adhere.

If you do not clarify such policies/procedures in advance, TAs will turn to other, and sometimes less reliable, sources for information. We have heard many stories about how TAs in a certain department have perpetuated myths about grading within the department. In one case, we heard stories in which TAs reported that they knew they were supposed to keep the class mean for final grades at a C+. Unfortunately, such a belief was a myth among TAs and handed down from year to year but never substantiated by a supervisor or other departmental administrators. In the worst case scenario, we knew of a TA who not only adhered to such a standard in grading but told his students, as he handed back assignments, that the reason some of them got lower grades was that he had to set the mean at a C+ because the department "frowned on TAs who graded leniently." In this case, of course, the undergraduates perceived that the grading policy was unfair, that the TA had little control, and that they would receive low grades no matter how much effort they put forth. You can help TAs avoid such unpleasant experiences by making sure that they know of any such policies in advance, and that they have strategies for informing students about such policies.

All TAs who grade must be informed about what to do about suspected academic dishonesty. Although policies vary from department to department and university to university, it is safe to say that issues related to cheating and plagiarism are not only disheartening but fraught with potential legalities. Students have clear due process rights, and TAs should understand that they cannot simply confront a student about cheating, make the accusation, and subsequently give the student a "zero." Legal precedent suggests that, at least initially, issues of academic conduct must be separated from issues of grading. Students must be informed of the concerns expressed about their work; and, in most cases, the specific university will have a formal process through which students accused of academic dishonesty must proceed. Therefore, TAs who grade should be informed at the outset what the policies and procedures for suspected academic dishonesty are. A good rule of thumb is that TAs should bring such cases to you first before they take action. Then, you can help them sort out the difficulties of a particular case. Problems often can be averted by discussing such issues when assignments are given and helping students to understand what is acceptable. Because of the complexity of the issue, however, it is imperative that you provide opportunities for TAs to discuss the challenges of academic dishonesty in their grading of student work before they actually begin to grade student work.

Provide Opportunities for TAs to Practice Consistency in Grading. To be fair to undergraduates, TAs must, either on their own or with the help of the supervisor, make decisions about how points for an assignment will be distributed, when students will receive partial credit, and so on. Again, these are decisions that TAs should make before beginning to grade. Although it is easy to tell TAs that consistency is important, they cannot always anticipate what it means to think about issues of consistency in advance of actually grading an assignment.

TAs report that it is helpful to have sessions in which experienced and less experienced TAs work with a supervisor to practice applying criteria. In some instances, you might talk about criteria for evaluating problem sets, for example, and then have all TAs practice applying the criteria to the assignment. In this case, it is useful for less experienced TAs to hear you and the experienced TAs talk about how you graded the assignment, how you determined when to give partial credit, and so on. Similarly, you can provide opportunities for TAs to practice applying criteria to the grading of papers, journals, lab reports, and essay exam questions. In some cases, you might ask TAs how they think consistency in grading can be achieved.

Using Additional Supervisory Strategies

Throughout this chapter, we have suggested areas where TAs need specialized training and some ways that you can assist TAs. Now we want to turn more specifically to some of the training strategies that you can use to prepare TAs for the challenges of the different instructional roles.

Use Trigger Situations to Provide TAs With a Variety of Instructional Strategies. Because there is no right way to teach, instructors, and particularly new instructors such as TAs, need to have a broad repertoire of instructional strategies so that, as they make instructional decisions, they can choose and implement strategies that are the most appropriate for themselves, the content, and the students. Trigger situations of the studio critique or the section leader asking questions to facilitate discussion, for example, are a useful way to provide TAs with strategies that they can use in their teaching.

The format for using trigger situations requires that you create a situation similar to one that is typically problematic for TAs, such as a student coming to the TA to challenge a grade or a student dominating class discussion. You can identify many of the problematic situations that TAs will face in their roles and then find a way to capture those situations. You might write them up in a short case, have a couple of experienced TAs role-play them, or actually develop a videotape that enacts such encounters. A key to the process is to use the situation only as a "trigger," to stop the interaction at a crucial decision-making point and engage the TAs in a discussion of what they would do or have them role-play the situation to a resolution. The goal is for you and the TAs to identify several different strategies that might work to address the issues in the trigger situation.

Once you have identified a number of possible strategies for use in a trigger situation, you should provide opportunities for the TAs to practice with a strategy of their choice. There is a big difference between saying they are going to use a particular strategy and actually being able to implement it. The TAs need to experience the on-the-spot decision making and subsequent challenges that can arise during implementation. TAs report that trigger activities help them to think about a variety of strategies, particularly when they hear what the supervisor and other experienced TAs have to suggest, and that the practice is particularly useful for thinking about what they will actually say as they carry out specific strategies.

Use Ongoing Meetings. A frequent complaint from undergraduates about courses that have office hours, labs, field trips, or sections associated with them is the lack of coordination between the courses and the part of the course for which the TAs are responsible. Students are quick to express their concerns that "the faculty member and the TA do not communicate" or that "the labs (or field trips) don't have anything to do with what we are learning in the large class." In the same way, students complain when there is inconsistency across labs or sections or office hours for the same course.

A major responsibility for you, then, is to coordinate the instructional roles, particularly for TAs whose responsibilities are extensions of courses you teach, so that the relationship between your work and the TAs' responsibilities are clear or so that there is consistency across the labs, field trips, office hours, and so on of the course. The most effective way that we know to achieve such communication and consistency is to hold ongoing—typically, weekly—meetings with TAs. Such meetings can serve a variety of important purposes. They can provide opportunities for you to identify important course goals that you are trying to accomplish so that the TAs can emphasize those goals in their varied roles. The meetings can also give you an opportunity to hear where TAs are encountering difficulties in working with the content or the students and give you the opportunity to help them generate approaches that they can use to address those challenges. Finally, such meetings provide the opportunity for you to obtain feedback both about how the TAs are doing in their roles and about what you may be accomplishing as the instructor in a large course.

Require That TAs Attend Large Class Lectures. Ideally, TAs who have instructional roles that serve as extensions of a large class (sections, labs, office hours, grading) you are teaching should attend the class you teach. Then, they can hear firsthand how you talk about goals, establish requirements, and emphasize information. They also can be prepared to explain difficult concepts in different ways and work through problems or examples that are different from the ones students have heard in the large class. One precaution, however: For many classes, the 3 to 5 hours per week that TAs spend in class should be counted as part of their assignment. Therefore, requiring them to attend the large class lectures always has to be balanced against their time commitments and the complexity of their instructional assignments/roles.

Use Microteaching. Microteaching (Allen & Ryan, 1969) is the use of videotaping combined with feedback from peers and a supervisor/consultant to enhance the teaching of TAs or faculty. During the process, participants teach, analyze, and reteach using videotape. In advance of the designated day, they prepare a short teaching segment in which they can practice instructional skills such as explaining a course on the first day of class, demonstrating a concept, using examples, balancing an equation, providing design critiques, or responding to student questions. Then, on the day of the microteaching, they videotape the short (micro) segment of teaching, usually 5 to 10 minutes, play back the tape, comment on their own teaching in the segment, receive constructive feedback from others in the group, and then reteach the segment to apply what has been learned.

Microteaching requires that you plan carefully. First, it is important to consider the goals for microteaching. It works best with TAs when it is intended to provide support, build confidence, develop instructional strategies, practice instructional language and methods, and/or identify specific areas for further practice and development. The levels of experience of the TAs and their instructional responsibilities will determine which goals are most appropriate. It also is important that you allow plenty of time for the process. Even when the reteach is saved for a later follow-up session, the process of videotaping, playing back, providing feedback, and assisting TAs in setting goals and identifying strategies for change requires, at a minimum, 30 minutes per TA. Because of the time involved, microteaching often works best with a facilitator and four to five TAs.

Because any videotaping can be intimidating, particularly for beginning TAs, it is important to use the microteaching process in supportive ways. You can achieve this goal by explaining the process clearly to the TAs well in advance of their participation, including what they are supposed to do to prepare, what they can expect during the process, and what they can hope to gain from their participation. One approach that seems to reduce risk is to have the facilitator and other participants assume the perspectives of undergraduate students to focus on what the presenter did that really was helpful and what could have been changed to assist them in learning. A strategy that works well during the discussion of each presenter's teaching is to allow the TA being videotaped to be the first to comment on the teaching once the videotape has been played back. It is often useful to guide the discussion with careful word choices, such as "What *worked?*" (as opposed to what was done *right*) in the TA's effort to achieve instructional goals and "What *changes* (as opposed to focusing on weaknesses) can be recommended?"

Finally, because of the value of microteaching as a training tool, it is a good idea to require participation. Most TAs will not participate if given an option. Once they do participate, however, they readily endorse the process as an instructional development tool.

In the words of one participant: "I was pretty nervous/skeptical going into it, but it was really quite excellent for helping me think about specific things I could do to make my teaching better."

TAs report that they like microteaching because it:

- Allows them to see themselves in action
- Lets them compare themselves to others
- Generates specific ideas they can use in their own teaching
- Helps them recognize that there is not just one way to be successful
- Provides the basic goal-setting for ongoing teaching improvement

In this chapter, we have identified a variety of instructional roles that TAs might fulfill and strategies for preparing them for those roles. Within any of the instructional roles, it is important that you identify the training that the TAs need and generate a variety of specific activities designed to prepare them. For additional ideas on ways that TAs can improve their teaching, you can refer to *Improving Your Classroom Teaching* (Weimer, 1993b), which provides helpful strategies for both you and the TAs. Using such resources to see that TAs have necessary skills not only assists the TAs in carrying out their present and future responsibilities but also saves you time and helps you avoid some of the most serious problems of working with underprepared TAs.

6

Preparing Graduate Research Assistants for Their Responsibilities

Preparing graduate student researchers for their assignments is similar to that of preparing teaching assistants (TAs) (Chapter 5), but it presents special challenges. Research assistants (RAs), like TAs, benefit greatly from understanding the expectations of the department and the professor with whom they work, and from being informed of the criteria by which they will be evaluated. Because research appointments are so varied, we decided to supplement our own experience by interviewing graduate student researchers and supervisors across a wide variety of departments in preparation for writing this book.[1] Quality supervision can and should be provided to RAs, of course, but our findings suggest that both supervisors and graduate students feel that adequate supervision is lacking in important ways. In this chapter, we have tried to address some of the issues they raised by looking at the skills needed by RAs. RAs must acquire the competencies required of their assignments, such as the following:

- Literature review approaches
- Sampling and data collection techniques

- Data recording methods
- Team member and collaborative skills
- Report writing processes
- Ethics and safety policies

Although we have had to approach these competencies in a general way, you can think about the specific skills your RAs need to do the kind of work required by your particular discipline and the current research being conducted in your department. You may want to use a matrix similar to the one suggested in Chapter 5 for assessing TA roles to identify the skills needed by your RAs (see Figure 6.1). Filling out such a matrix will help you to decide where to spend time in training.

Again, list the names of your RAs in the left column and check off the various skills they will need to acquire to be successful RAs. Depending on the results of your assessment, you will need to teach basic skills in each of the needed categories. In addition, RAs need to be supported by their supervisors as they progress toward being professionals.

Compiling Literature Reviews

RAs often begin their appointments by conducting a review of the literature that grounds the research project. Sometimes, this review frames the work and needs to be exhaustive; other times, especially if a grant has been awarded, the original literature review was completed at the time of the proposal submission, so the RA is simply checking to see if any more recent work in the area has been published.

Whatever the case, RAs need to be given time and instruction, often provided by library personnel, to learn to use library resources in an efficient manner, including database search methods, and so on. Even if an RA has done extensive searches previously, he or she must learn the procedures at your institution. Such reviews of literature often provide RAs with a helpful background and context for the work you intend to assign.

Name	Literature Searches	Sampling and Data Collection	Data Recording Methods	Team Member Skills	Report Writing	Ethics and Safety Procedures
1.						
2.						
3.						
4.						
5.						
6.						
7.						
8.						
9.						
10.						

Figure 6.1. Skills Needed by RAs

Sampling and Data Collection

Obviously, sampling techniques vary widely from discipline to discipline and depend upon the specific research project. RAs, particularly those new to a program, need to learn the processes expected of them whether in the library, in the laboratory, or in the field. Projects vary from archival investigations for projects in history to salmon restoration monitoring in Ocean and Fisheries projects to collecting traffic information in Civil Engineering, to name a few examples, each using different data collection procedures. The RAs we interviewed repeatedly suggested that faculty supervisors across disciplines not only must explain clearly the way they want the sampling done, but also that they need to go into the library, laboratory, or field with the RAs to demonstrate how the process should be performed. We were told frequently that supervisors need to experience the difficulties of fieldwork and not remain armchair researchers, ignorant of the pragmatics involved and sometimes requiring the impossible given the RAs' other responsibilities to their courses and their families.

For example, RAs were quite critical of supervisors who send them out without a clear sense of what to do, and of those who order more samples than can ever be analyzed. RAs interpret that experience as wasting their time and as an act of disrespect on the part of the supervisor.

There are many issues in data collection beyond sampling, of course. How data should be collected, whether by telephone or personal interview, archaeological dig, survey questionnaires, water samples, library searches, checking of tagged species, or numerous other processes is often a personal, idiosyncratic decision made by the individual faculty member or principal investigator on a grant.

You can help your RAs, then, by making clear your expectations, setting workable deadlines, accompanying them and actually participating in the collection of data by demonstrating your approach from time to time, and by checking frequently on their progress. RAs often can be of great assistance in designing sampling techniques, contributing to your project and to their own growth.

Recording and Reporting Data

As with data collection techniques, methods used for the recording of data are often personal preferences of the principal investigator or otherwise stipulated by the grant. Whatever the case, RAs need to know how the decisions were made concerning the reporting of data, and they need to be given models of what you expect the final product to look like. As RAs mature and become junior colleagues, it is important to engage them in decision making whenever possible. Because they are the ones actually handling the data, they often become excellent critics of both sampling and reporting procedures. Listening to your RAs carefully will often identify new, efficient procedures that you, as supervisor, have not thought about. In turn, such interactions will contribute to the growth and development of the RAs as they move toward becoming professionals.

Developing Team Member Skills

Because much of current research is conducted in research teams, especially in the natural sciences, and because potential employers are often critical of our graduates, whom they label as individualistic and competitive rather than collaborative, RAs need to be prepared to work with others in meaningful and productive ways. As a supervisor of RAs, you will need to lead the team. Because working with others requires skills typically not tested in BA or BS programs, you may need to spend time addressing such issues as division of labor between team members, relationships between and among team members, and collaborative work.

As you divide up work on a research team, you must be sensitive to how your RAs are interpreting the assignment of tasks. For example, you may regularly give one member of the team the review of literature process because you can count on that person's thoroughness and completion of the task on a timely basis, allowing other members of the team to go forward with their particular duties, which are dependent upon the initial review. If the graduate student to whom you routinely give such an assignment interprets it as a less difficult and challenging position than that given to other members of the team, that team member will be disappointed and may attribute your decision to a lack of confidence in his or her abilities. Expectations for each team member should be made public to the rest of the group in order to make all contributions valued and, hopefully, as equal as possible. The issue of giving credit for the more mundane tasks remains a challenge, but clearly, even a manuscript that will be submitted to a prestigious journal will require careful proofreading by a knowledgeable person. Someone must do it, and it is a time-consuming, nonglamorous, but essential obligation. Think carefully about how you make assignments. If you are approaching your RAs from a developmental perspective, you will make opportunities for each of them to stretch to the next level of performance.

You, as leader of the team, must also set the priorities. Assuming that RAs know immediately how their time can be best spent is risky; after all, you are the one who has the "big picture" in mind and should be the one to determine which assignments are most important to be completed on an agreed-upon timeline. At times, team members will not be able to complete their assignments if they need to build upon the work of others that has not been completed. Such delays create dissension among the team members.

You may need to spend some time demonstrating and giving examples of the kinds of collaborative processes in which you intend the team members to participate. If you plan to have a postdoctoral student lead the team in your absence, then you need to transfer that responsibility publicly.

Remember that graduate students come to your project to work with you and, if the daily routine is other than that, such an arrangement must be understood by all involved. Otherwise, the postdoctoral student will encounter resistance from team members. Again, because employers complain about our students' deficiencies in the area of working collaboratively to solve problems, you may want to be particularly careful about how you set up the teams and how you equip RAs to function on them. The RAs will most likely take into industry or into their future supervision experiences in higher education the models you provide. Sometimes, it is useful to have someone from departments of organizational management or communication function as a consultant to bring to the attention of your RAs what is known about teamwork and leadership. A potential employer often can come to campus to address these issues in a most convincing way.

Writing Reports for Publication

Most of the RA supervisors we interviewed wished that their students could write better. We certainly feel the same way. But lamenting the lack of writing skills does not help you or the RAs. Again, we have found that a developmental approach works best. Based on our interviews, an effective RA supervisor divides up the writing tasks into a progression that enables RAs to work through all the writing assignments that will be required of them as professionals.

First, our supervisor does not call steps in a study "research" until the results are written up. Thus, to be viewed as researchers, all of her RAs must write. Her students begin by selecting from a current research project five articles from the literature review to read and critique in one paragraph each. These critiques are brought to and discussed at a regular meeting of all her RAs during fall quarter. She reads and responds to their critiques of the articles with the goal of having them learn how to assess in written form various research articles. This allows her to evaluate their writing competency early in her relationship with them. She also assigns, on a rotating basis, the first draft of the monthly and quarterly reports on the grant for the funding agency. She returns RAs' drafts with comments and a copy of what she actually submits and entertains questions about why she made certain decisions in the final draft.

A second assignment she gives her RAs is to require them to write a grant proposal for the grant that is funding them; she then has them compare their work to the original proposal that has been funded. She makes it a point to have her RAs identify distinctions between the various funding agencies and their requirements, especially those appropriate to the RAs' interests. She emphasizes the competitive aspects of grant writing, insisting that the students' proposals must provide a unique reason that will ensure acceptance (e.g., a way to squeeze out other proposals at the National Science Foundation).

Our supervisor also has her RAs prepare a grant proposal in their area of interest that usually goes through seven or eight revisions. A few that show particular promise are then coauthored by her, rewritten until acceptable, and actually submitted. She also requires that her graduate student advisees identify as early as possible papers from their dissertations that have the best potential for publication.

In addition, when our supervisor is reviewing articles for a journal, she often has her RAs write a review to compare with what she has written. Sometimes, she has her RAs evaluate essay tests or papers from her undergraduates if she is dealing with appropriate concepts in her classes. Then she evaluates their evaluations.

Third, our supervisor reports that she spends time helping her RAs deal with issues of authorship in an explicit way. In her discipline, the convention is that the faculty member is always last author, even if she has done the majority of the work. She routinely invites two graduate students to coauthor with her and leaves to them the working out of who will be the first and second author. She discusses openly those decisions, hoping to assist her RAs to practice making those arrangements for their later professional lives.

Although we found this supervisor's thoughtful ways of supervising to be unusual and extremely effective for her RAs, we were concerned about the enormous amount of time and effort that she expends to provide such a training program. She believes, however, that the investment pays off in the quality of dissertations she receives and in the opportunities for coauthorship that such a collaborative relationship provides. Clearly, students benefit from her supervision, both in their current work and in their development as professionals.

Considering Issues of Ethics and Safety

In addition to the above issues, there are, of course, those important aspects of ethics and safety. Supervisors must ensure not only that their graduate student researchers develop technical research skills, but also that they confront squarely issues of ethical conduct: the careful handling of research data, replication of study information, validity and reliability tests, patents, and so on. Contemporary science has, unfortunately, come under vigorous attack for not being conducted in ethical ways. The faculty supervisor must not only model ethical conduct but also assume responsibility for ensuring that what goes on in research projects and in laboratories meets all of the professional standards for inquiry and publication, including protection of animals and so on. Recent charges of falsifying data have seriously damaged the academy's reputation for doing pure science and require explanation and discussion so that such unfortunate activity can be avoided.

In the social sciences, supervisors, in addition, must ensure that human subjects are protected and that all requirements are met for research on and about humans. Graduate student researchers must have the opportunity to learn about the process of human subjects reviews. Human subjects review committees work somewhat differently on each campus, but learning the requirements and paperwork required of an institution during one's time as an RA will allow the student to know which questions must be asked at their new institutions. Meeting his or her current institution's requirements is equally as important to the supervisor, of course, and again, this is the responsibility of the supervisor. Indiscretion on the part of the RA must be answered by the supervisor. He or she is ultimately responsible!

Likewise, the supervisor is responsible for issues of safety. Graduate student researchers not only must be versed in standard laboratory safety requirements, but also must be trained to be constantly vigilant in terms of risk of humans and/or equipment. Whatever policies are put in place, the supervisor must by his or her own conduct model those policies and require that others do likewise. Any dangerous substances or experiments need the direct supervision of the supervisor. Such important information—safety policies—must appear in both oral and written forms to lessen any possibility for miscommunication.

Practicing Supportive Supervision of RAs

However you provide for the development of the skills outlined here and those that are peculiar to your discipline, RAs need support as they master those skills. If you make assignments according to their development (as suggested in Chapter 3), you can expect to see RAs systematically and incrementally acquire the needed research competencies and the attitudes of a researcher; and they will benefit from your support as they move through that process.

Support can be given through a variety of interactions with RAs. Many of the RAs we interviewed reported that their interactions with their supervisors were too infrequent and insufficiently structured to meet their needs. Although how one becomes a first-rate researcher depends primarily on an individual graduate student researcher's basic curiosity and resourcefulness in solving problems, RAs report that supervisor interest and guidance are keys to their development. The interviewees suggested that weekly meetings, often lasting no longer than 30 minutes, during which the supervisor calls for status reports, deals with schedule conflicts related to graduate coursework requirements, and makes public decisions and what lies behind them, are immensely helpful.

In fact, sharing out loud how you think is crucial to RA development. As mentioned earlier, professional competence requires making unique judgments about completely novel cases; this cannot be taught. Such competence must be gained by being exposed to effective models. Students will learn both positively and negatively from you as they developmentally construct their professional selves. However, the best role models do not clone themselves; instead, they provide their novice researchers with ways of thinking about research challenges. New graduate student researchers do need to be exposed to literature review approaches, sampling and data collection techniques, data recording methods, team member and collaborative skills, report writing processes, and ethics and safety policies. But this is not sufficient for the development of a professional. RAs need to know how decisions about the research process are made, beginning with the initial idea, the proposal, the data collection and/or manipulation phases, through to the analysis and publication of the results and their significance. How the experienced researcher thinks about each of those steps is critical to the development of a beginning researcher.

The best research models talk openly about the decisions behind the decisions; the times that they were just lucky and discovered something by accident on the way to investigate something else;

the options they considered and rejected; the times they were undecided; the times they made wrong decisions that cost them much in time, money, and energy—mistakes that sometimes were even costly to their reputations. Effective role models can talk about the cognitive processes that precede action in the research process; about the indecisions, the doubts, and regrets; and about the questioning of their own priorities and motivations. From those conversations, RAs learn of the complexities and tensions of conducting quality research and of the risks, sometimes painful, that make up the excitement and opportunities involved in doing research. They also learn about the humans who do such work. Experienced researchers appear confident and assured; RAs need to know that what is on the surface does not always represent the whole picture so that they will see as normal their own misgivings and apprehensions about their work.

To ask a supervisor to provide all this may seem like too much is required, but the task of preparing the next generation of researchers for industry, government, and higher education is a high calling, indeed. It demands our best efforts.

Note

1. Special thanks go to Professors Krieger-Brockett and Stuve of the University of Washington for their many helpful ideas. They are most thoughtful about their supervisory roles.

7

Addressing Special Considerations When Working With International Teaching Assistants

Gabriele Bauer

Universities attract talented individuals from around the world, and international graduate students contribute significantly to the instructional and research mission of most universities in the United States. Given this growing internationalization, you are likely to supervise graduate teaching assistants (TAs) from abroad. At first, you might have concerns similar to those articulated by one faculty member: "I am concerned about my role in supervising a graduate TA from Malaysia. She is most knowledgeable in the discipline, but she has not taught before and seems to be very shy. I am not sure how to assist her. Where do I start? I don't know much about working with international students." A good place to begin might be the kinds of approaches you are using already to prepare American TAs. Such approaches are also relevant to assisting international TAs (ITAs) in their specific instructional roles (Chapters 1 through 5).[1]

As a supervisor, I encourage you to prepare ITAs and American TAs together for their instructional responsibilities so that each may benefit from the experiences and diverse perspectives of the other. The goal of this chapter, however, is to familiarize you with some special challenges that ITAs are more likely than American TAs to encounter in their teaching roles and to offer suggestions for assisting them with these challenges. Key issues include:

- Assumptions about the role of TAs
- Familiarity with American educational settings
- Familiarity with interactive teaching approaches
- Interpretation of undergraduate student behavior
- Teaching in a nonnative language and communicating with students
- Perceptions of undergraduate student feedback

This chapter closes with some recommendations for preparing international graduate student researchers who, like ITAs, can be assisted in some specific ways. These suggestions expand on the issues raised in Chapter 6.

In addition to the suggestions mentioned in this chapter, I encourage you to investigate any central ITA preparation program on your campus to learn about the kinds of services the program offers and then decide how to expand and supplement these with departmental training activities. International TA program curricula generally focus on three areas: the improvement of ITAs' English language proficiency for instructional purposes, the facilitation of intercultural communication skills, and the enhancement of ITAs' teaching effectiveness (Smith, Byrd, Nelson, Barrett, & Constantinides, 1992). The programs vary in content and design: Most start with an orientation prior to the beginning of the academic year and continue, to varying degrees, with specific courses or individualized consultations throughout the year. For example, some universities offer extensive summer programs for prospective ITAs, whereas other institutions integrate ITAs into a general orientation for all TAs immediately preceding the fall term.

ITA programs offer not only an essential resource for ITAs but also a unique opportunity for your department to collaborate with the ITA program (refer to Tanner, Selfe, & Wiegand, 1993, for an example of such a collaborative ITA training effort). ITA program staff are also familiar with print and video resources that address the specific needs of ITAs, which you might find helpful in your supervisory role. Numerous reference materials are also available to help you broaden your knowledge of other cultures (e.g., Culture-grams produced by Brigham Young University, print and video resources offered by the Intercultural Press).

Assumptions About the Role of TAs

Although the TA role is uniquely characteristic of the American higher education system, ITAs interpret this role based on their own cultural frame of reference. For instance, Craig, a TA from Canada, anticipated that he would grade students' homework problems and meet individually with students if they wished to do so. He described his expected contact with students as minimal. To his surprise, he was asked to conduct three problem-solving sessions per week with 25 students each. En-Jia, a TA from China, perceived her role as having complete responsibility for a class. Based on such perceptions, she chose the textbook, designed the course, and determined assignments and grading criteria without prior contact with her faculty supervisor. She was surprised to find a memo in her mailbox inviting her to join the faculty member and fellow TAs to talk about the course and the TAs' responsibilities. Both examples illustrate how important it is for both you and the ITAs to clarify role expectations and to inform ITAs about their responsibilities.

An initial meeting with the ITA gives you the opportunity to learn about his or her perceptions of the teaching position and to describe carefully how the position might be similar to or different from what the ITA anticipated. You might indicate your role in the course and describe not only how the ITA's role complements yours as the course instructor, but also how it contributes to undergraduates' learning. You might outline also the expectations that American students have of the TA role. For example, ITAs need to know that students perceive the TA as a link between themselves and the professor, as someone who is approachable, available for questions, and responsive in helping students to think and learn. American undergraduates often perceive TAs as individuals who are easier to approach than the course instructor. Mere discussions of these expectations with the ITA are not sufficient, however, and ITAs need firsthand experiences with American students to internalize some of these expectations.

You can help ITAs describe their roles to the students in various ways. You can invite ITAs to your first class session and introduce them to the entire class. You might talk about those aspects of their academic background that are relevant to the course, and you might describe how ITAs will contribute to the class. You might consider addressing the TA responsibilities in grading, conducting office hours, and holding review sessions. Your positive and precise statements about the TAs' responsibilities will positively influence undergraduates' attitudes toward the ITAs (Bresnahan & Kim, 1991). As one ITA mentioned, "When the course supervisor stated that I was not responsible for grading the students' studio projects, but that I was available to help them with their individual projects, I was relieved. Her introduction gave me credibility and made me comfortable interacting with the students in the studio."

In addition, you can help ITAs think about how to introduce themselves and describe their responsibilities when they meet the students for the first time. One supervisor, pretending to be the student, role-played the situation with the ITA and provided the ITA with instantaneous feedback about her introduction. The ITA then revised her introductory statement based on the feedback. Experienced TAs can give similar feedback. Another faculty member encouraged the ITA to design a syllabus for his discussion sections and to outline his role in the document. The ITA wrote: "The section is a direct complement to the lectures. My role in this section is to help you explore and clarify some of the issues that are central to this course. We will do so by discussing actual cases. I will also help you better understand marketing concepts by linking them to practical situations in the case analyses. In short, I am here to help you."

Familiarity With
American Educational Settings

International TAs have been educated in instructional settings that are somewhat different from the American context, and they bring varied cultural backgrounds, and thus educational models, with them. These experiences provide you as the supervisor both unique assets and challenges. Although ITAs contribute to the diversity of the campus community and offer students, faculty, and staff tremendous opportunities for intercultural contact and learning, they may be unfamiliar with American classroom settings and hold models of teaching and learning that are not appropriate. A questionnaire can help you learn about the various backgrounds and experiences that ITAs bring to their graduate instructor appointments and thus may reveal their educational exemplars so that you can adjust them if necessary. Questionnaire items might address the following topics: native country, native language, prior visits to the United States, familiarity with the American educational system, perception of language proficiency, prior teaching experience in the home country and/or in the United States, and instructional concerns. Appendix A offers a sample questionnaire that you might use to identify ITAs' prior educational experiences and current needs. Some TA coordinators mail the questionnaire to ITAs in conjunction with the appointment letter. Then, they incorporate this information into their planning for both departmental TA training activities and individual supervisory relationships.

To help familiarize ITAs with specific instructional contexts as well as undergraduates' expectations, you might include opportunities for practice teaching in your departmental TA training schedule. For example, a microteaching format allows ITAs to practice their teaching in front of undergraduate students and graduate peers. It is important that you include undergraduates in the microteaching process because they serve as an authentic audience regarding an ITA's instructional language, cultural awareness, and teaching approach. Frequently, undergraduate majors in the department are interested in participating in such a process. To model the interactive nature expected in instruction, students ask questions during the presentation. After each presenter comments on his or her videotaped performance, the audience members provide immediate feedback on classroom communication skills, classroom interaction, and cultural aspects. In the discussion, you might focus on aspects of nonverbal communication, clarity of presentation, use of questions, response to students' questions, use of transitions, and paraphrasing. Such constructive criticism from students and peers is the first step in helping ITAs monitor their teaching effectively. As one ITA states, "Microteaching in my department was most helpful. I could actually observe what I was doing, get feedback from undergraduates and other TAs, and then reflect on the information." In Appendix B, you will find a sample form that might be helpful to you in preparing ITAs for a microteaching session as well as in discussing the practice presentation with them.

You also need to provide ITAs with practice during their actual teaching assignments because they often do not control the content or topic of discourse in the classroom. The laboratory setting offers such a challenge for many ITAs. They are expected to move around, interact with the students, ask questions, and take initiative. They need to explain the procedures of the experiment, explain and enforce safety regulations, operate the equipment if necessary, manage time and people, ask questions, and formulate answers (Myers, 1994). To assist TAs in chemistry, for example, the TA supervisor designed the following practicum. All TAs who taught introductory organic chemistry conducted the actual experiment a few days before they needed to do it with their students. The course supervisor was present at the lab practice and provided assistance. The practice entailed setting up the equipment, designing the prelab lecture, announcing the safety procedures, conducting the experiment, anticipating the kinds of questions students might ask, and storing the lab equipment. This practice is helpful in several ways: ITAs work side by side with native-English speakers, and they receive informal feedback about their instructional language, about laboratory tasks, and about difficulties that students might encounter. TAs are thereby trained to develop strategies for responding to these issues.

Familiarity With
Interactive Teaching Approaches

ITAs need to adjust to an instructional setting that tends to be different from the one in their home countries. Most ITAs come from educational systems with minimal interaction between instructors and students. Students tend to participate in class as listeners and note-takers (Pica, Barnes, & Finger, 1990). In the United States, ITAs find themselves in smaller classroom settings where interaction is expected and where students prefer an informal, personalized, and supportive classroom atmosphere (Nelson, 1991).

Most of the instructional roles mentioned in Chapter 5 do require some kind of interaction with the undergraduates. Consequently, the American classroom potentially can become a site for intercultural misunderstandings. When I asked ITAs what they found to be most challenging when they tried to engage students in class, they identified using examples appropriate to undergraduates' experiences and responding to students' questions as difficult challenges.

Using Appropriate Examples. Because ITAs are often unfamiliar with the cultural and educational background of the students, they find it difficult to integrate relevant and interesting examples into their teaching, particularly those with which undergraduates are familiar. Examples illustrate abstract concepts, support theories, personalize instruction, and improve student learning of the content. Student feedback further indicates that those ITAs who include interesting and relevant examples in their instruction are perceived as effective in helping students comprehend the material and in establishing rapport. Many ITAs have difficulty locating other sources for examples besides the textbook. As supervisor, you can assist ITAs in developing examples by referring them to their own cultural background and experiences. When ITAs personalize the lecture content via use of personal examples from their own cultural background, students tend to be more attentive (Nelson, 1992). Questions such as "How would you explain this to a person in your home country?" or "What personal or professional experiences have you had that might relate to this theory?" might help ITAs perceive their own cultural background as a resource. Tat, an ITA in business, used his own travel experiences in Japan as an example to talk about customer service in department stores in Japan in contrast with department stores in the United States. He also supported his story with slides that showed Japanese salespeople bowing at the door to welcome customers. According to one student, "I found it interesting when Tat brought in his own background to what he taught. His examples made the class more enjoyable and memorable for me."

In some departments, TAs have collected folders of examples that worked well in particular courses and have made them available for use by all TAs. You might suggest various print and video resources that you have found helpful in selecting timely examples for your courses. You might also encourage ITAs to draw from their students' knowledge during class, and ask them to bring in relevant examples. Strategies such as these will enliven the teaching and learning process for both ITAs and their students.

Responding to Students' Questions. Unlike the lecture setting, for which ITAs can plan ahead and present the material accordingly, interactive settings are less predictable. Students' questions add an element of the unexpected and can become a source of anxiety for ITAs. You need to consider ITAs' cultural assumptions about the nature of students' questions. In some educational systems, instructors are perceived as authorities in their fields, and they are expected to have mastered the content of their disciplines. For example, one way in which Chinese students show respect for their instructors is by not interrupting their presentations with questions. Students' questions are viewed as rude interruptions that demonstrate disrespect on the students' part, and most instructors do not encourage them (Hudson-Ross & Dong, 1990). As one ITA pointed out, "I am surprised by some of the questions undergraduates ask. They ask me about things that were explained in the readings. They obviously haven't done the readings and seem to ask uninformed questions. Do I need to respond to them?"

You need to describe the role that questions play in learning and teaching. In the American academic culture, students' questions are perceived as opportunities for learning because they exemplify a desire to know and to check understanding. International TAs' engagement in practica, such as the laboratory described earlier, can help them anticipate students' questions. You can also team the ITA with an experienced American or international TA in the department who has taught the course before and can serve as a mentor. In such a role, the experienced TA could share the kinds of questions that undergraduates typically ask. The practicum setting also provides a safe environment for ITAs to practice possible responses to students' questions that they do not know how to answer. A question I have been asked frequently is, "What do I do when I cannot respond to a student's question? I will lose credibility in front of the class. What do I say at that moment?" You might need to explain that, contrary to the ITAs' educational experiences, students do not expect instructors to know all the answers. Students expect the instructors to find the answers and bring them to class the next period, or to explore the question together with the students. You might help ITAs increase their repertoire of possible responses in this uncomfortable and potentially embarrassing situation. Statements such as these offer alternative ways to provide students with an initial response: "I am not sure, but I will definitely find out and let you know." "I am sorry I do not have an answer for you right now, but I will get back to you tomorrow." "What do we already know that would help us respond to Jane's question?"

In addition to ITAs' interpretation of the nature of students' questions, you might consider ITAs' familiarity with the academic backgrounds of college students. As one ITA mentioned,

> I completely overestimated the students' ability. When I read the textbook, I assumed that they would be bored. The material seemed basic to me. So I prepared additional problems to solve in the quiz section. Based on students' questions asked in the quiz section, I realized that my problems were much too difficult. I needed to adapt to the students' level and also prepare various ways of explaining a concept.

ITAs might find it similarly difficult to gauge the knowledge of their students. Many of them are unaware of the level of knowledge that undergraduates bring to college, especially in the languages, sciences, mathematics, and engineering. To help familiarize ITAs with students' backgrounds, you might inform them about the level of preparation an instructor can expect of students in a particular course. What have students learned in high school? What do high school science curricula look like? With which course materials might they already be familiar? What gaps in their knowledge and skills could you expect? What courses are prerequisites? Are the students freshmen or seniors? You might also suggest to ITAs that they learn about students' backgrounds, expectations, and reasons for taking a specific course. One TA asked her students about their TV viewing habits and their favorite TV shows. She used this information to provide examples at a later part of the course on the effects of mass media.

Interpretation of
Undergraduate Student Behavior

Differences in cultural backgrounds between undergraduate students and ITAs have an impact on their daily instructional interactions and offer potential for misinterpretation of student behavior. For example, one ITA talked with her supervisor about the dwindling numbers of students in her problem-solving section. She was concerned about the students missing class and wondered what the reasons might be. Her explanation was that the students did not seem to be serious about their education and seemed to have little interest in the course material. When the faculty supervisor asked her, "What makes you think so?" she replied, "That's how I would interpret the students' behaviors at home." Similarly, in class discussions, it is likely that students will voice their opinions, which may diverge from the TA's. ITAs, again using "behavior from home" as their guideline, might read the disagreement as a sign of disrespect undermining their credibility in class. As a supervisor, you can recognize these situations as opportunities to learn about the ITAs' cultural assumptions and help them to recognize cultural differences.

For example, you might offer your interpretation of the situation and encourage the ITA to talk with experienced TAs as to how they respond in similar circumstances. Written case scenarios, role-plays, and videotaped trigger situations that portray potentially challenging classroom situations are resources you might use to help ITAs interpret student behavior from an American cultural context. Examples of such encounters are a student questioning the ITA's grading policy during class or office hours, students talking with each other during a pop quiz, students neglecting safety procedures in the lab, and so on. Experienced ITAs can assist in constructing discipline-specific, realistic scenarios.

Many ITAs come from educational backgrounds that are characterized by a formal instructor-student relationship. They expect students to behave formally in their verbal and nonverbal instructional interactions. Students, on the other hand, expect some degree of informality in the classroom. Office hours and tutoring sessions lend themselves toward informality, which can sometimes be awkward for ITAs. Strategies to break the initial discomfort and tensions might need to be considered. Small talk using phrases such as, "Good to see you," "I'm glad you could make it," "How are things going?" and "How have you been?" helps put students at ease and provides a gateway to content-oriented issues. Any examples that demonstrate informality between instructors and their students are most helpful to ITAs. You might consider several sources for such examples: commercially produced videotapes such as the one offered by the Harvard Teaching Series titled *Teaching in America: A Guide for International Faculty* (1993), videotaped examples of excellent teaching in your discipline, or actual classroom observations of experienced TAs.

Instructional tasks, such as responding to questions, clarifying assignments, solving problems, and practicing language skills, also demand a supportive, encouraging instructor role. Students expect to be acknowledged and recognized for their valuable contributions in the class. Undergraduates tend to be fairly sensitive to criticism and might perceive an ITA's comment more negatively than intended. For instance, "This is an easy problem," can be interpreted not as encouraging but as demeaning of the undergraduates' efforts. Several ITAs have mentioned to me that based on their own educational experience, it is the instructor's role to tell students when they are wrong but not to reward them for what they do right. If the instructor does not say anything, that is because the answer is right, and there is nothing to add. The undergraduates, on the other hand, tend to interpret the ITA's lack of encouragement as lack of caring for their learning. In your role as a supervisor, it is crucial to inform ITAs about student expectations and to engage them in conversations with experienced TAs and ITAs.

Teaching in a Nonnative Language and Communicating With Students

As nonnative speakers, many ITAs are concerned about their use of English in the classroom setting. Such concerns range from pronouncing English words correctly to understanding the students' language and responding to their questions (Bauer, 1992). As one ITA said, "I am concerned about my language. The students may misunderstand me and then get lost." To assist ITAs who experience difficulties communicating in class with their undergraduates, consult the expertise of English as a Second Language (ESL) professionals and ITA trainers at your institution. They are familiar with methods and materials that ITAs will find helpful. Typically, ESL programs offer specific courses, individualized language assistance, native-English-speaking conversation partners, and conversation groups.

Some ITAs find it helpful to inform their students that they are nonnative speakers of English. They acknowledge that initially students might find it difficult to understand them, and they encourage the students to let them know when this occurs. One ITA jokingly referred to her students as "my dictionary," and the students willingly and supportively took on this role. Another ITA mentioned that in addition to talking with undergraduates about his language, he gave them written lecture outlines and handouts. The students followed the handouts in class and had no difficulty understanding what he was talking about. In addition, he used e-mail to post students' assignments and to respond to students' questions. In short, the undergraduates had various means, besides oral communication, to clarify their understanding. Similarly, you might introduce your ITAs to various media to support their oral presentations, such as the use of overhead transparencies and the board.

Several ITAs have indicated that as second language speakers, they feel reluctant to correct the written work of native speakers. In a recent conversation with Kunihiko, I learned that he had spent the entire week correcting his students' papers. He felt he had to be extra careful with his written feedback and provide lots of explanation for why he corrected what he did. When he returned the papers to the students, he discovered that he had given them too much feedback, and students were overwhelmed with the information. In addition, he realized that his feedback was inconsistent with what had been provided by TAs in other sections. In your role as a supervisor, you might need to ask ITAs how much experience they have had grading written assignments and whether they felt comfortable doing it. In addition, ITAs might not be familiar with the conventions used to indicate word choice, tense, or word order. You might familiarize ITAs with the conventions you expect them to use by working with sample student papers. After a general discussion of these conventions, you might ask ITAs to apply them when correcting sample papers. These papers might be exchanged and discussed further to determine consistency of application.

Perceptions of
Undergraduate Student Feedback

Most ITAs who have no prior experience as students in the American educational setting are surprised to learn that student feedback is an essential source for assessing an instructor's teaching effectiveness. Initially, ITAs might be uncomfortable with receiving feedback about their instruction from undergraduates, but they might be reluctant to bring it to your attention. Their discomfort with student feedback might be rooted in their cultural experience that only faculty peers are credible sources of feedback. To illustrate, one ITA wondered why students were put in a position to question the instructor's authority, credibility, and knowledge. Another ITA linked amount of knowledge to assessment. She felt that the students might not know enough about the discipline to assess the instructor's effectiveness accurately.

The feedback that ITAs most commonly encounter comes in the form of student ratings, which they are required to distribute to their students at the end of the term. Quite often, ITAs learn about this mandated student perception measure only shortly before they are asked to distribute it in class, which in turn produces anxiety. You can help reduce some of this anxiety by introducing ITAs to the role and value of student perceptions prior to their TA appointment. For example, a supervisor in a language department uses a session during the departmental fall TA training program to discuss the topic of student ratings. Experienced TAs cofacilitate the session with her and provide their perspectives of how they have used the ratings to reflect on their teaching methods and to make changes. They can address explicitly the cultural differences that student feedback processes represent. They also share actual examples and help novice TAs work with the numerical and qualitative information. The session also provides a forum for novice TAs to voice their concerns and get their questions answered within a supportive environment. Furthermore, the collegiality developed in the session tends to continue throughout the year with TAs sharing and discussing their ratings with each other.

Another opportunity for such discussion might be an initial meeting with ITAs. You might start with a general overview of student ratings information, such as the long-standing tradition, the validity and reliability of such measures, and their contribution to the assessment of instructional quality as one source of feedback but not the only one. You might then proceed by showing ITAs the actual forms that they will use and by describing the kinds of information these forms provide. Regardless of the format, you need to define how student ratings are used in your department and what role they play in ITAs' reappointments. You might structure your conversation around such questions as, "Are ratings used for diagnostic, improvement-based purposes?" "Are they used for determining the continuation of an appointment?" "Are they confidential in nature?" "Who has access to the information?" "Will the ratings become part of an ITA's file?" "Will the ratings be discussed with the TA?" "Are there certain levels at which TAs are expected to perform?" A discussion of such questions also allows ITAs to voice their concerns openly, minimizes potential misunderstanding, and helps reduce anxiety.

When ITAs receive their ratings, you might arrange a meeting to discuss the data with them. To help involve ITAs actively in the interpretation process and to encourage them to reflect on their teaching, you might ask them to identify strengths and areas for change prior to the meeting. For example, one supervisor asked ITAs to write a reflective essay about their end-of-term student ratings. Specifically, he asked them to use the course goals and learning objectives outlined in the syllabus as a framework for the essay. In the next step, ITAs described how well they felt they had met these objectives, offered examples, and discussed what they would do differently next time. Finally, they compared their own perceptions with those of their students. The supervisor used the reflective essay as a starting point for the conversation and then incorporated his own perspective. Approaches such as the one described provide the ITAs with multiple sources of feedback about their instruction, and they help increase the ITAs' awareness of their instructional approaches, a necessary skill for professional growth.

You can also encourage ITAs to incorporate ongoing student feedback in their particular instructional contexts. Ehud, an ITA in international studies, asked his students to provide him with feedback on the class discussion in their weekly journal entries. The students responded to the following questions: "What did you learn as a result of the discussion?" "What worked for you in the discussion?" "What did not work for you and how can it be changed?" He used the entries to modify the discussion format to better meet the students' learning needs. In his words, "I was taught by my students how to structure and facilitate an engaging and productive discussion."

Preparing International
Graduate Student Researchers

So far, this chapter has introduced you to some of the key issues you might consider as a supervisor of graduate students who teach. Many international graduate students also hold research assistant (RA) positions and might have been recruited to the university for their research potential in the discipline. The issues raised in Chapter 6 regarding your supervisory relationship with RAs definitely apply to your work with international RAs. Two special considerations emerge regarding international RAs: clarity of expectations and reluctance to ask questions.

Clarity of Expectations. In many academic settings, the quality of scholarly activities determines the success or failure of a professional career, and thus many graduate students aspire to research positions in their respective fields. When the position is provided, RAs rely primarily on their own cultural backgrounds to interpret this role. As one RA expressed, "I look forward to my RAship. I can work independently on a project that is assigned to me and see it through to the end." The RA did not anticipate any faculty involvement in the project and was quite surprised to learn that not only did the supervisor participate in the project, but he was also expecting the RA to report to him about progress. The RA was understandably disappointed in her research assignment because of her inaccurate faculty expectations.

It is essential to clarify the expectations that accompany both the RA role and the supervisor's role. Similar to your work with ITAs, you might discuss these expectations during an initial meeting with your RAs. You might present the RA roles within the context of the particular project and describe how the RAs are expected to contribute to the project. You might ask RAs to describe their assignment in their own words so that you can clarify any potential misunderstanding. One supervisor, for example, approached the task by asking the RAs to write a brief reflective statement about what they hoped to gain from the RA experience. The supervisor then used the statements to start the discussion of role expectations and to clarify inaccurate perceptions that were held by RAs. Another supervisor used the first meeting to identify the knowledge and skills the RAs already brought to the research project (e.g., library skills, writing skills) and then indicated which skills they needed to develop during the project (e.g., computer skills, interviewing skills, and discourse analysis skills). She also reassured the RAs that she would provide the resources necessary to help them acquire these skills.

Reluctance to Ask Questions. Based on their cultural background, some RAs are reluctant to inform you when they encounter difficulties or experience frustration. They perceive it as their responsibility to find a solution to the problem and invest as many hours as necessary to correct it. As one RA stated,

> When I run into a problem, I do not tell my supervisor. It is up to me to solve it. I look for library resources, I study written materials, and I redo the experiment as many times as needed. My professor is the last resort. I hesitate to talk with him because he might think that I am not qualified to conduct the research.

You might help RAs with such concerns in several ways: You might meet with them on a regular basis, you might ask them to provide written progress reports, you might work with them side by side in the lab or at the computer terminal, or you might reassure them that some difficulties are likely to occur when conducting research and that it is your responsibility to assist them to complete their research assignments. Also, remind RAs that you are ultimately responsible for the project and thus need to know when obstacles arise so that you can assess the difficulties and make appropriate corrections and adjustments with their help.

Whenever possible, work with RAs on new tasks. One supervisor laments,

> I explained a new computer program to my RA and asked her whether she had any questions about it. She said no, she was okay with it. When I returned a few hours later and walked up to her, I noticed that she had not started the program. When I asked her whether she needed any help, she declined politely. At this point, I was not sure what to do next to help her.

In similar situations, I have found it helpful to sit down at the computer with the RAs, to go through the actual process with them, and to guide them with questions such as, "How do we access the program?" "What do we need to do as the first step?" "What do we do next?" and "What does this symbol stand for?" Questions such as these change the focus from performance to collaborative, discovery learning. You might also ask RAs to work together on new tasks, to help each other as equals.

Your supervisory relationship with international graduate students allows you to enhance and reward intercultural contact, thereby improving departmental morale. You can do so by inviting ITAs to share their cultural heritage and educational experiences, which, as a bonus, will help you become more cognizant of your own cultural background. However, the challenge for today's educators is to create and offer an academic environment in which students learn to respect and appreciate people from different cultures and backgrounds. The task is complicated but worthwhile.

Note

1. The term *American* as used here refers to both undergraduate and graduate students who are U.S. citizens and are enrolled at institutions in North America.

APPENDIX A

Questionnaire Regarding ITA's Background

To help me get to know you better and respond to your individual needs as an international teaching assistant, please complete this questionnaire and mail it back to me (my departmental address is on the back). Your responses will be treated confidentially. Thank you for your time, and I look forward to meeting you soon.

1. First Name:	Last Name: (family name)
2. Sex: □ female □ male	

3. Native
  country:
	4. Native
	  language:

Please answer the following questions about your intercultural experience:	

5. Have you traveled in any foreign
   countries?
	□ yes, where? _____
	  for how long? _____
	□ no

6. Have you studied in any foreign
   countries?
	□ yes, where? _____
	  for how long? _____
	□ no

Please answer the following questions about your teaching experience (if you have not taught before, please answer question 7 and skip to question 14):	
7. Have you had any teaching experience?	□ yes □ no
8. In which *countries* have you taught?	□ Home country □ U.S. □ Other _____
9. What *grade levels* have you taught (check all that apply)?	□ Elementary (grades K through 6) □ Secondary (grades 6 through 12) □ Four-year college/university □ Other _____

| 10. For *how long* have you taught (check one)? | ☐ less than 1 yr.   ☐ 3 to 5 yrs.
☐ 1 to 2 yrs.   ☐ more than 5 yrs. |

11. What *subject areas* have you taught?

12. Describe your teaching situation. What instructional approaches have you used in your teaching (e.g., lecture, group work, writing?)

13. When you think about teaching undergraduate students at this university, what are you most concerned about and why?

    I am concerned about . . .

Please answer the following questions about your English fluency (if you are a native speaker of English, please skip to Question 17).

14. For how many years have you studied English? _____

15. Overall, how would you rate your ability to communicate in English?
    ☐ very good   ☐ good   ☐ fair   ☐ poor

16. How comfortable do you feel speaking English?
    ☐ very comfortable   ☐ somewhat comfortable   ☐ not comfortable

We would really appreciate your answers to the following additional questions:

17. What do you hope to gain most from participating in the departmental TA training program?

18. Please use this space for any questions or comments.

Please return this form to:
Departmental Address

APPENDIX B

First-Day-of-Class Presentations (Microteaching Worksheet)

Preparation for Presentation

In this session, you will present a 5-minute presentation focused on the first day of class. You will be videotaped, and once all the presentations have been recorded, we will view the tapes as a group. This technique allows you to determine how well you achieve your instructional goals in a short teaching segment. After you watch the videotape, we would like you to share with the group what worked well for you in the presentation (i.e., please indicate things that worked for you and that you would do again). Following this, you will be asked to share what things you would change or do differently if you were to do the presentation a second time.

As you watch your presentation, consider the following questions: (a) Was my presentation clear? (b) Was it organized? (c) Did I use an introduction? (d) How did I use the board? (e) Did I maintain eye contact with the audience? (f) Was my voice clear and easy to understand? (g) Did I try to interact with the audience? (h) Did I establish rapport with the audience? Overall, did I achieve my instructional goals?

Analysis of Videotaped Presentation

Part I: (To be completed as you view the videotape)	Part II: (Group comments)
A. What worked well for you in this presentation?	A. What worked well for you in this presentation?
B. What would you change or do differently next time? How would you do this?	B. What would you change or do differently next time? How would you do this?

8

Assessing the Performance of Graduate Teaching Assistants and Graduate Research Assistants

Assessing how well teaching assistants (TAs) and research assistants (RAs) fulfill their roles is one of the most important, yet most often slighted, parts of the supervisory process. TAs and RAs suggest that they want to know what is expected of them and appreciate constructive feedback that will assist them in meeting expectations. Departments need information regarding TA/RA performance for reappointments and assignment of responsibilities. Yet when we ask TAs and RAs how they are evaluated, they report too often that the process is a mystery that has never been adequately explained or carried out with them. Therefore, this chapter is designed to help you think about ways to make the assessment of TAs/RAs work for everyone involved.

Organizational literature reports that employee performance is enhanced when appropriate and fair assessment procedures are in place so that employees and supervisors share the same performance expectations and understand the criteria by which success will be judged. It is to the advantage of the department to seek the highest levels of performance from the teaching and RAs. For TAs/RAs, input from a variety of sources can help them to determine how they are doing and what they need to do to improve—such input helps in their growth as individuals and professionals. For you, a good assessment program provides a way to monitor the quality of the TAs'/RAs' work and to assess their development as future faculty/scholars or professionals. However, these advantages can be achieved only in a carefully planned, comprehensive program. The following guidelines are offered to assist you in thinking about how best to establish such a comprehensive program for the TAs/RAs you supervise.

Guidelines

Clarify Assessment Purposes. Two typically important purposes of assessment are to help individuals improve and to determine whether they should be retained in their roles. You must decide, then, whether the evaluation will serve only one of those purposes or both. As we have suggested in previous chapters, because TAs/RAs are simultaneously progressing through stages of development, there are developmental issues that you should consider. The key is to select goals appropriate for the needs of the department and the level of development of the TAs/RAs, and then to clarify the purpose(s) for the TAs/RAs. The approach always requires a careful balance of expectations with appropriate follow-through support.

Provide a Written Summary of the Assessment Process. One way to clarify the expectations and support available is to put assessment expectations in writing so that TAs/RAs can review them at any time. The summary might be included in orientation materials as a separate document or as part of a departmental or supervisor handbook. At the minimum, it should reinforce the importance of the TA/RA role in the department and of the use of feedback in helping TAs/RAs fulfill their roles. For example, it might simply begin with a statement like:

> TAs are important in our department. They are directly involved in classes/laboratories with more than X (number) undergraduates

each term and interact with approximately another X (number) through written comments, office hours, and so on. Our department recognizes the crucial instructional role that you play and stresses the importance of your having the information and resources that will assist you to be successful. One way to provide such information and resources is to make sure you are involved in a comprehensive program of assessment. This brief handout is designed to provide the essential information about the assessment program that your supervisor will use, including the ways feedback will be gathered, discussed with you, and used by your supervisor and the department.

For RAs, a similar statement might be adjusted slightly to read:

In our department, RAs serve important roles as research assistants who work with faculty to achieve research goals. More than X% of our graduate students serve in research roles in which they conduct literature reviews, gather data, analyze and write up results, and work closely with a faculty members in all stages of the research process. Our department recognizes the crucial research role that you will play and stresses the importance of your having the information and resources that will assist you to be successful. One way to provide such information and resources is to make sure you are involved in a comprehensive program of assessment. This brief handout is designed to provide the essential information about the assessment program that your supervisor will use, including the ways feedback will be gathered, discussed with you, and used by your supervisor and the department.

The summary should describe how information for the assessment process will be collected, reported to the TAs/RAs, and used by the supervisor or department. Also, you can include information about relevant assessment policies, including policies related to racism, sexual harassment, code of conduct, ethics, and plagiarism. Although it is important to clarify these aspects of the assessment program, you simultaneously should remain sensitive to needs of the TAs/RAs for support as they think about all parts of the assessment contract.

Present the Description of the Assessment Process in a Supportive Atmosphere. Too often, graduate students report that supervisors forget the importance of being supportive. "Being evaluated" only increases the level of stress for many beginning TAs/RAs. Thus, you should reinforce that graduate students do succeed and survive in their roles and that you and the department will do everything possible to support them. Help TAs/RAs to understand that the evaluation is a process of gathering information about how they are doing and providing lots of opportunities for them to learn to do better. You also can reinforce the idea that you know they are learning their new roles and that initially they cannot be expected to know everything. Furthermore, it is useful if you can arrange activities so that they can hear other TAs/RAs talk about how it feels to be facing new challenges and experiencing feelings of inadequacy.

Involve the TAs/RAs in the Assessment Process. TAs/RAs often view assessment as something that is "done to them," or imposed from the outside. Although that sense may be true, it does not have to be. It is possible to include the TAs/RAs as active participants in several different parts of the assessment process. As we suggested in Chapter 4, you can begin by viewing any information that you gather as data and by including the perceptions of the TAs/RAs as one important source of such data. You also can include the perspectives of the TAs/RAs in interpreting, or making sense of, the data and, most certainly, in deciding how to act on it. Including the perspectives of the TAs/RAs in these ways moves you from the role of "evaluator" to the role of confederate and allows the TAs/RAs to feel that they have a voice in the improvement of their teaching or research and in their ongoing development.

Provide Feedback About Both Strengths and Areas for Change or Improvement. Powers (1992) discusses two different kinds of feedback—motivational and developmental. Motivational feedback "reinforces good performance" and "acknowledges people for doing what you want them to do" (p. 135). Developmental feedback, on the other hand, "is intended to help participants develop or correct their performance" (p. 136). Powers goes on to suggest that although both are used "to reinforce and develop excellent performance," motivational feedback is appropriately given in either the public or private setting, whereas developmental feedback is intended only for the individual and, therefore, should be given confidentially.

These distinctions serve as important reminders that you can always begin such feedback sessions by discussing strengths but that at some point it is imperative—even though you may feel uncomfortable doing so—that you discuss the areas in which change is needed.

Establish Goals, Strategies, and Follow-Up Procedures. A comprehensive assessment program does not end with providing motivational and developmental feedback. Rather, it moves beyond the feedback to goals and strategies and, eventually, to ways to follow up on efforts to achieve those goals.

For this part of the process, we use an open-ended worksheet like the one in Figure 8.1 to record ideas as they are discussed. We begin by asking the TA/RA a question like, "Out of this feedback, what is of the greatest interest or concern to you?" Then, we listen as the TA/RA begins to identify concerns. We try to help him or her clarify those interests and concerns and provide guidance in his or her thinking, particularly about the areas that are the most important in his or her assigned role. Allowing the TA/RA to identify areas of interest and concern provides another way to emphasize the role of the supervisor as confederate and, again, gives the TAs/RAs a sense of some control over their own assessment.

We then invite the TA/RA to identify three or four of the major interests or concerns that he or she would like to address. For lab instructors, those goals might be something like, "to provide more explicit directions for lab experiments" or "to ask questions that encourage lab partners to seek their own answers." For RAs, sample goals might be "to increase the number of times calculations are recorded" or "to keep a better record of tentative hypotheses as results are recorded." It is important to help TAs/RAs establish goals that you agree can make a difference without creating undue stress or focusing TAs/RAs on their teaching or research at the expense of their progress as graduate students and scholars. Typically, three or four goals are adequate for TAs/RAs to work with at one time.

Once goals are established, you are ready to talk about specific ways or strategies for the TAs to accomplish the goals, and ways to follow up on accomplishment of the goals. Discussion of strategies should help the TA/RA choose those with which he or she will feel most comfortable and provide him or her with specific methods for

Concerns	Goals	Strategies	Follow-Up

Figure 8.1. Feedback Worksheet

implementing the strategies. Once you have determined that the TA/RA has sufficient strategies and ways to implement them, you can move to ideas about follow-up. You might, for instance, conduct another observation in the laboratory to determine whether you think the TA is providing more explicit directions for laboratory experiments. Or, for the RAs, you might check from time to time to see if he or she really is able to use strategies you discussed to increase the number of times that calculations are recorded. The process of gathering data, analyzing it, setting goals, following up, and then suggesting new goals creates a cycle that requires ongoing efforts.

Establish Assessment as an Ongoing Process. The number of times that you actually review their materials or observe TAs or RAs and then meet with them is limited by your other responsibilities as a teaching scholar/researcher and by the number of TAs/RAs you supervise. Nevertheless, as part of the process, you will be continually helping TAs/RAs move through the cycle that includes trying to achieve present goals and setting new goals each time present goals are achieved. In addition, ongoing assessment will allow you to address the needs of TAs/RAs at different stages of their development. As the graduate students move through various phases of their development, their needs and expectations, and, subsequently, their goals for improvement, will vary. Your way of adapting to those variations is to work with assessment of the TAs/RAs as an ongoing process with data gathering points spread across time.

Use the Assessment Process to Obtain Feedback That Can Help You as the Supervisor. As we mentioned earlier in this chapter, the assessment process provides an opportunity for you to identify areas for further training. In some ways, the information you obtain about TAs/RAs is a collective reflection of the quality of your supervision. Through data from your observations, interactions with TAs/RAs, their own self-report, and students' perceptions of TAs, you can obtain information that will help you identify areas in which TAs/RAs are clearly succeeding and areas in which they need further guidance. For example, when one professor we knew tried to prepare TAs to work through problems with students in sections, she was pleased to observe during follow-up that they were involving students in the thought processes as they worked problems in the sections. Simultaneously, however, she observed that the TAs generally were not incorporating ways of assessing whether students can do the same kind of thinking on their own. As a result, in future training sessions, she needed to spend time helping the TAs think about assessing students' understanding in the problem-solving sections. In the same way, you may find in working with RAs that they are now applying specific methods that you have recommended in their analysis of data but are struggling with ways to display data in the most succinct and useful ways. Therefore, you may need to develop follow-up training sessions to assist RAs with methods for data display.

You can also use individual and group meetings to obtain feedback about what TAs/RAs need. Informally, you can ask them what you are doing that is helpful and what you could do differently to assist them. More formally, you could distribute feedback forms and ask TAs/RAs to provide feedback about a specific training session (Figure 8.2) or about the overall assessment program used during the quarter/semester (Figure 8.3).

The feedback forms do not have to be elaborate or time consuming for TAs/RAs to complete. They just need to provide specific information that will be helpful to you.

Sources of Data
About TA/RA Effectiveness

As we discussed in Chapter 4, assessment works especially well when you can think of it as a process of collecting data to make instructional decisions. There are a variety of ways to obtain the data for the assessment of TAs or RAs. Although some sources are more appropriate for one role than the other, it is only fair to the TAs/RAs that you try to include as many different perspectives and approaches as feasible within the constraints of your job, particularly because each approach only presents one part of the total picture. To assist you, we have included in Figure 8.4 a diagram representing possible sources of data for assessment.

We have focused the next part of this chapter on some of those sources of information, including self-perceptions of TAs/RAs; perceptions of supervisors, peers, and administrators; and student data sources—student perceptions and student performance indicators.

Self-Perceptions of TAs/RAs

We recently observed in the classroom of a TA who, as part of an ongoing student project, was asking groups of students to conduct information-gathering interviews with professionals in the commu-

Session Response Form

1. The information presented in this meeting was clear and well organized.

strongly disagree	disagree	agree	strongly agree
1	2	3	4

2. The information/skills training was relevant to my needs.

strongly disagree	disagree	agree	strongly agree
1	2	3	4

3. I feel I can use the information or skills training immediately in my research (or teaching).

strongly disagree	disagree	agree	strongly agree
1	2	3	4

4. Overall, I think the session was valuable.

strongly disagree	disagree	agree	strongly agree
1	2	3	4

5. What part of the session was most useful?

6. What are some of the areas in which you would like additional information or assistance?

7. Other comments about the session:

Figure 8.2. Feedback Form for Specific TA/RA Training Meetings

Response Form—Assessment Program

1. Expectations for the assessment program were clearly explained.

strongly disagree	disagree	agree	strongly agree
1	2	3	4

2. A variety of helpful sources were used to obtain input about my teaching (or research).

strongly disagree	disagree	agree	strongly agree
1	2	3	4

3. My supervisor was effective in providing feedback during the assessment process.

strongly disagree	disagree	agree	strongly agree
1	2	3	4

4. The assessment process helped me determine what I could do to improve my teaching (or research).

strongly disagree	disagree	agree	strongly agree
1	2	3	4

5. Overall, I think the assessment process used this term was useful.

strongly disagree	disagree	agree	strongly agree
1	2	3	4

6. What part of the assessment process has been most helpful?

7. How could the assessment process be changed to be more helpful to you in your research (or teaching) role?

8. Other comments about the assessment process:

Figure 8.3. Feedback Form for the TA/RA Assessment Program

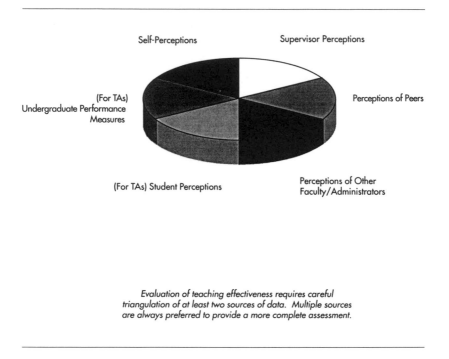

Self-Perceptions

Supervisor Perceptions

(For TAs)
Undergraduate Performance
Measures

Perceptions of Peers

(For TAs) Student Perceptions

Perceptions of Other
Faculty/Administrators

*Evaluation of teaching effectiveness requires careful
triangulation of at least two sources of data. Multiple sources
are always preferred to provide a more complete assessment.*

Figure 8.4. Sources for Evaluating the Effectiveness of Teaching
Assistants and Research Assistants

nity. When we observed in his class, we noticed that he was rather
indecisive about whether he should take class time to discuss the
groups' progress with their interviews. He said near the end of the
class, "I have more that I want to tell you, but maybe we should
stop now so you can talk a little about how your interviews are going.
(pause) Or, do you need time to discuss your interviews?" The students sat quietly and glanced around at others in their assigned
groups; a few shrugged. We started making written and mental
notes: For what we know about undergraduates' need for structure,
is the TA being too nondirective? Is he creating unnecessary tension
about their not receiving vital information that they will need for
future assignments? Then, when we discussed our observations
with the TA, we addressed these issues: "We noticed near the end

of the class that you told the students you had more to tell them but that you wanted to see if they needed to spend some time discussing their interviews. Can you talk a little bit about what was happening there?" The TA explained that on the previous day he had discussed with the students anonymous feedback that he had asked them to write about how the course was going. He said some students said that they needed class time to ask him questions and discuss their interviews with other members of their groups. Others wrote that he sometimes spends too much time "dragging out the discussion" about their interviews. So, in an effort to address their concerns, he had discussed with the entire class the issue of using class time to talk about the interviews. They all agreed that an appropriate solution would be for him to ask them from time to time whether they need to talk about their interviews. What we learned by including his perceptions before we jumped in to make recommendations was that the students were expecting his nondirective approach.

As the previous example demonstrates, we have found it useful in our work with assessment of TAs/RAs to include their self-perceptions as one source of data. In addition to giving them a voice in the assessment process, including their perspectives provides valuable insights for a supervisor. You will learn why they make certain choices and how you can best help them with the choices they make.

Most of the time you can obtain the perceptions of the TAs/RAs through questions in your discussion with them. If you are using a written evaluation form with them, however, you might have them fill it out for themselves before you meet with them for feedback. Then, you will have information about how they perceive their effectiveness for the specific items on which you have rated them, and you can use their ratings as a springboard for discussion as you fold your perceptions into the discussion.

Supervisor Perceptions

Your own perceptions will be useful for both motivational and developmental feedback because you will be the one most directly involved with the activities of the TAs/RAs. One potentially useful source of information about the work of either TAs or RAs lies in the materials they produce. For TAs, you can review such materials as syllabi, worksheets, assignments, visual aids, or samples of graded papers, lab reports, problem sets, or exams. Review of materials is especially helpful for assessing the effectiveness of TAs who are in tutoring/office hours or grading roles, where some of the other sources of data are not feasible. For RAs, you may obtain samples of literature reviews, summaries of research designs, journal entries, records of calculations, written summaries, displays of data, or progress or final reports. The review of such materials with RAs is particularly important because other sources of data for assessment, particularly sources related to students, are not available.

Depending on how closely you work with the TAs/RAs, you may see their materials frequently anyway. If not, it is a good idea to suggest to the TAs/RAs that you want to see examples from different phases of their work; then they can anticipate and retain the most relevant examples. To save time, you can ask for specific materials in advance of the actual discussion with the TA/RA. Then you can review the material before a meeting with him or her.

The approach in assessing materials does not have to be particularly formal. In fact, TAs/RAs will be most at ease if you can just engage them in a good discussion about the materials they submitted. You can begin by seeking their perceptions of the materials and then raising questions about issues that interest or concern you. In the cases where you have established certain criteria that they must meet in their syllabi or research journals, however, you can develop a checklist or ratings form that you can use to review with them the extent to which they have met the criteria.

Another way to develop the perceptions for the assessment process is to observe the TAs/RAs at work. Although observations will be useful regardless of whether you supervise TAs or RAs, there will be differences in the way you conduct observations for the two roles.

Observations of TAs. The instructional observation provides a way for the supervisor to visit the instructional settings where TAs are interacting with students, make observational notes about the instruction, and later meet with the TAs to discuss what was observed. Such observations are especially appropriate for TAs who have responsibilities in classroom, laboratory, or studio settings.

Although observations require lots of supervisory time, they also provide a perspective that TAs and supervisors cannot obtain from TAs' self-perceptions, and they open the way for discussions that will allow TAs/RAs to take advantage of your knowledge and experience as a faculty member and/or researcher.

To use instructional observations as important elements in a TA training program, you should consider the following:

- *Instructional observations may require an initial meeting between you and the TA.* Because teaching effectiveness is contingent on an instructor's ability to achieve worthwhile instructional goals with a particular group of students, it is important that you understand in advance what a TA is trying to accomplish in a given session. Even when TAs are teaching a section, studio, or lab that is directly related to a larger course that you are teaching, and even when a group of TAs is trying to achieve the same instructional goals in similar ways, a preobservation conference is helpful for setting the stage and obtaining the TAs' perspectives on what will be observed. Furthermore, a preobservation conference provides an opportunity for you to review expectations with the TA and relieve some of the anxiety that TAs report they feel when they know their supervisor is going to observe them.
- *You may use either forms with open-ended categories or ratings instruments to obtain data.* You can observe, for instance, with questions as open-ended as "What is working to help the TA achieve the instructional goals?" and "What could be changed to assist the TA in achieving the instructional goals more successfully?" If you wish to write comments in categories that are not quite so open-ended, you may use general categories that have been identified in the teaching effectiveness literature or, for example, in Weimer's (1993b) volume on improving classroom teaching: instructor knowledge, organization, student engagement, rapport, and classroom communication. For instructors who prefer to observe with checklists, a number of interaction analysis systems or forms have been developed for purposes of colleague evaluation (Braskamp & Ory, 1994; Powers, 1992; Seldin, 1985).
- *It is important to obtain information that can be useful for the TA in thinking about ways to improve.* We have found it particularly useful to obtain data that describe, rather than evaluate, what we observe, and data that later can help us and the TAs be reflective. In the final stages, the observational process should include a postconference in which you

and the TA discuss the data, including both your perceptions and those of the TA, and move toward decisions about goals for improvement, strategies, and approaches for follow-up.

- *Videotape can be used in a particular kind of instructional observation that is sometimes called a videotape critique.* The videotape critique involves arranging for videotaping of a TA's instruction and meeting with the TA to view the videotape and discuss what has been recorded. Using a videotape in this way allows you greater flexibility. If you cannot observe at the time of the scheduled class, the class can be videotaped, and the critique can be scheduled for a convenient time. A major advantage of using videotaping in this way is that it provides views of the classroom instruction that can be used, saved, and retrieved for later review. In addition, being able to watch themselves demonstrate effective behaviors through the use of videotape can be extremely reinforcing for TAs (Nyquist & Staton-Spicer, 1987).

Despite its strengths, videotaping presents some particular challenges of which you should be aware. Unlike the observation, the videotape critique has the logistical burden of scheduling video equipment and working out details of getting undergraduates' permission if they are going to appear during the interaction recorded on the videotape. An additional challenge in the use of videotape is the selectivity of the camera—it can never really capture all that is happening in a classroom.

Nevertheless, TAs report that even though they are initially hesitant about being videotaped, some of their best training experiences are provided by opportunities "to see themselves in action." So, once you decide to provide them with the opportunity, there are a number of steps that you will want to consider when using the videotape critique in your assessment program. First, unlike the classroom observation, video critiques do not necessarily require a preconference between you and the TA because you can obtain his or her perceptions just before viewing the tapes. But, in advance, you should decide whether it would be helpful for TAs to view the tapes individually before they meet with you for their critiques. Such a procedure often relieves anxiety and allows them to eliminate some of the initial negative reactions that many of us experience when we see ourselves on videotape for the first time. In some cases, you may want them to select segments to focus on as a way of saving time. Once you meet with the TA to discuss the tape, review procedures for the session and have the TA talk about goals for the instructional session that was videotaped. Then, again beginning with initial reactions from the TA, you can focus on the questions of what seemed to work and what could be changed to enhance student learning in the segment. When there are areas that you perceive as problematic that the TA does not identify, such questions as "What were you doing here?" or "What were you thinking here?" can be extremely helpful (and far less intimidating) in focusing the discussion on some of those issues. In fact, you will discover that you are more successful in conducting videotape critiques when you ask questions and listen carefully. As with other approaches, ultimately you will want to move the critique to a discussion of concerns, goals, strategies, and methods for future measurement of effectiveness.

Observations of RAs. As a supervisor of RAs, you will depend heavily on the observations of their work. In contrast to the observations for TAs, however, it is more likely that the observations of RAs will be conducted informally on an ongoing basis. As you work with the RAs in the laboratory or in the field, you will have opportunities to notice how effectively they organize their time, meet deadlines, solve problems collaboratively, set up experiments, obtain and record data, analyze and write up results, and work as team members. Similarly, you will have more frequent chances to give the RAs feedback as they progress. It is hoped that your schedule will permit you to take advantage of these opportunities, because RAs are very clear about the fact that such feedback gives them a sense that you do care about them and that you want them to learn.

If you provide ongoing observations for RAs, you should:

- Inform RAs from the outset that they will be observed on an ongoing basis.
- Identify in advance the specific evaluative criteria that you will use to assess their effectiveness.
- Reassure RAs that although it may seem that they are under constant pressure to perform well in your presence, because of the number of opportunities you will have to see them in action, they will have ample

opportunity to redeem themselves should they be struggling with the research role at some point during your observations.

- Consider the use of videotaping to help you be more efficient. Although a videotape critique typically is not practical for assessing the effectiveness of RAs, you may be able to use some form of videotaping as a data source if RAs have videotapes of themselves conducting interviews or gathering data in ways in which it would be feasible to videotape. Particularly if you use videotape to assess their interactions with subjects during interviews, however, it would be important to consider the ethics of subject confidentiality and any guidelines established by the Human Subjects Review Board or similar agency on your campus.

Perceptions of Peers

Research suggests that peers can be an important source of information for TAs (Darling, 1986; Staton & Darling, 1989). In fact, many TAs prefer seeking information from their peers (Duba-Beiderman, 1993). Although peer-related data may not be something that you would use directly in your interactions with TA/RAs, they are a source of data that TAs and RAs could use for their own improvement in their overall program of assessment. For instance, we knew a professor who supervised eight TAs teaching a basic course. Because she felt she could not conduct more than one observation for each per semester, she asked pairs of TAs to observe each other's class, noting what seemed to be working well and what the instructor might think about changing in such general areas as content knowledge, organization, instructional methods, and classroom interaction. She also asked each pair to conduct a postobservation discussion to review perceptions of what happened. She reported that although she did not always know what the pairs discussed in their postobservation sessions, the activity was extremely useful. TAs being observed reported that they received helpful feedback and a different perspective from someone who was trying to accomplish some of the same goals in his or her own class. TAs who conducted the observations reported that it was valuable to see a different teaching style and different ways of conducting the class. The professor herself was pleased to have provided this additional opportunity for TAs to be reflective about their teaching roles.

Because RAs sometimes work in small groups or research teams, they, too, can provide observational feedback as a way of helping each other improve.

Perceptions of Other Faculty/Administrators

Data from other faculty and administrators typically will not be a major source of information in your work with TAs/RAs. We mention it, however, because it could become relevant in a couple of different ways. It might come into play if, for instance, during your interactions with TAs, they bring in data from other faculty or administrators to add to the discussion. It might also be relevant if you have to figure out how to incorporate it in your overall program of assessment or if you have to summarize your data in ways that it can be compiled along with data from other faculty/administrators in an overall assessment of the TAs/RAs. The fact that others might be providing feedback simultaneously to the TAs/RAs you supervise suggests one note of caution: When you are initially obtaining perceptions from TAs/RAs, always include a question about whether there are related goals that they previously have been working to achieve, either goals that they may have identified for themselves or goals that they may have identified in working with others. That way, you can assist the TAs/RAs in developing their program of assessment as an ongoing, coherent process, building on any previous goals.

Student Perceptions of TAs

A useful source of assessment data that is available only for TAs is data based on students' perceptions. These data might be obtained for TAs in a variety of ways. Informally, they could come from feedback that the TA has solicited. At the end of a unit or a particular laboratory exercise, students might provide feedback about how the TA has assisted them in learning and what he or she could have done differently to assist them more fully. TAs might then compile a summary of such information for discussion with you.

Student perceptions also might be included from more structured sources. For example, on many campuses, a centralized instructional development center offers services that help TAs compile various kinds of student input for the improvement of their teaching. You might familiarize yourself with such services available to TAs on your campus and decide how to incorporate some of them in your program of assessment.

Another structured source of student perceptions, and by far the most common, is student ratings. On many campuses, TAs who assume teaching roles in sections, labs, studios, or courses in which they are the instructors of record are required to have students complete student ratings of teaching effectiveness. The ratings often include some kind of scaled items as well as written comments in response to open-ended questions. Summaries of these ratings are then available for review by the TAs, their supervisors, and department chairs. Although the form of these ratings varies greatly, they generally focus on teaching dimensions that have been established as important in assessing effectiveness and on items that students identify as important in response to open-ended questions about what is worthwhile in a course and what needs to be changed. Certainly, such ratings provide an important source of information that you can use in talking to TAs about the quality of their teaching. By glancing through the ratings summaries and students' comments to open-ended questions, you can begin to identify areas in which the TAs seemed to be successful and areas in which they need to make adjustments.

One thing to remember about student perceptions is that they represent one part of the total picture of a TA's instructional effectiveness. Although the ratings can be useful for helping you and the TAs understand whether students think they are learning and whether they think TAs are effective at imparting information, they are student *opinions*. The ratings cannot address important content issues such as whether the content is well chosen, up to date, or appropriately sequenced. In addition, students are not in a position to assess the overall development of a TA from term to term or year to year. For these reasons, although student perceptions can be a useful source of insights, other measures of effectiveness—the perceptions of the TAs themselves, your perceptions as one who works closely with the TAs, perceptions of faculty and administrators who work closely with the TAs in other settings, and student performance measures—are also essential to a comprehensive program of assessment.

Student Performance Measures for TAs

One important measure of teaching effectiveness is student performance—indicators of whether students are learning. Although one must be cautious about making definitive judgments about a TA's effectiveness based on student performance, there are ways to include student performance data in a comprehensive program of assessment for TAs. For example, if there are several sections of the same course taught by TAs and consistent grading procedures are applied across sections, you can determine if one TA's sections have class means on exams or assignments that are consistently higher or lower than those in sections for other TAs. In other cases, you might focus on student performance by inviting TAs to compile some samples of student work that demonstrate how individual students have improved performance. TAs in a variety of roles— from tutoring to assisting a professor to teaching a section—might demonstrate, for example, how they helped a particular student progress in the development of ideas for a paper, in basic writing skills, or in ability to solve problems or meet requirements of a laboratory write-up.

Although student performance data are potentially helpful, their use in the assessment process presents some particular challenges. You cannot establish direct links between teaching effectiveness and student performance because of the various factors that could affect student learning (background, simultaneous experiences in other classes, etc.). Thus, you may end up relying more on specific student products that include baseline data and reflect progress on goals that the TA was trying to achieve. More commonly, you will find you will have to rely on some of the other sources of data described in this section.

Clearly, there are many options for sources of data to include in your program of assessment for TAs/RAs. Although you will never be able to use all of them, you should try to obtain as complete a picture as possible on which to base your final assessments. This is the effort that makes your program of assessment comprehensive. Because the many different sources of information in a comprehensive program of assessment may come to you haphazardly, or perhaps because you may not have time to keep track of all these different sources of information for each TA/RA that you supervise, you may want to consider portfolios as a way of having TAs take responsibility for and organize their own data for assessment purposes.

Portfolios

Perhaps you have noticed in the recent literature on evaluating teaching much discussion of portfolios (Anderson, 1993; Edgerton, Hutchings, & Quinlan, 1991; Hutchings, 1993; Seldin, 1991; Seldin & Associates, 1993). For a long time, portfolios have been part of the world of artists and people in business, but increasingly, educational scholars have focused on portfolios as a way to address some of the challenges of the assessment process in higher education.

Portfolios are compilations of materials that reflect the quality of an individual's work. Seldin and Associates (1993) have described them as factual descriptions of teaching strengths and accomplishments that include documents and materials that collectively suggest the scope and quality of an individual's teaching performance (p. 21). In the case of TAs, a portfolio might include a variety of kinds of information that would help to assess the TA's instructional effectiveness. For example, it might contain a videotaped sample of teaching or other instructional interaction with students, summaries of student ratings or other forms of student evaluation of teaching effectiveness, or copies of syllabi, course materials, assignments, worksheets used during tutoring/office hours, or samples of students' work. For RAs, portfolios might include samples of literature reviews, journal entries, recordings of data, analyses, or write-ups of research.

There are a number of advantages to encouraging graduate students to use portfolios:

- They provide a variety of information that you can discuss with the TAs as part of their overall assessment and a way for it to be organized.
- They can add to the sense of control felt by TAs/RAs because the TAs/RAs are able to select the materials that they think best represent their development as instructors and research scholars.
- They provide TAs/RAs with experience that will be invaluable in future careers as faculty or researchers who must have performance evaluations conducted as part of their professional positions.

If you decide to use portfolios with the graduate students you supervise, it is important that, first, materials in the portfolios be tied to the accomplishment of specific instructional or research goals so that success can be measured against those goals. Second, authorities on the use of portfolios generally agree that portfolios should contain the artifact (syllabus, videotape, student ratings), a description of it, and some interpretation of its importance as evidence of effectiveness. Therefore, TAs should include, for example, not only a sample videotape but also a brief written explanation of background about the tape and comments that discuss how the tape demonstrates their instructional goals and their efforts to achieve those goals. Similarly, a sample data display for an RA should include not only the display but a brief description of it and an interpretive statement explaining what the display illustrates about the RA's effectiveness as a researcher. Such materials can provide an important springboard for your discussion with the TAs/RAs. Realize, also, that some of the materials that might best reflect effectiveness are artifacts that show how the TAs/RAs have progressed or developed skills over time. Thus, encourage them to save samples of their work. Even samples that reflect their struggles in initial attempts can be useful in providing baseline information. Finally, stress to graduate students that you cannot possibly attend to all of the materials that they might want to include in a collection that represents their teaching or research efforts. The key is for them to compile a variety of materials but to become adept at selecting for inclusion in the portfolio the few materials that best represent the quality of their work as instructors and/or researchers. Such selectivity is certainly a useful skill to be developed in the TAs/RAs with whom you work, and it will save precious time for you.

In this chapter, we have presented a synthesis of guidelines about developing a comprehensive assessment program for your TAs/RAs and identified some of the many ways that you might obtain and compile data that could help you in the assessment process. Although you probably could not single-handedly develop a comprehensive program of assessment that adheres to all these suggestions, we encourage you for your own sake, and for the sake of the TAs/RAs, undergraduates, and your department, to think carefully about what it means to develop a program that effectively assesses the performance of the TAs/RAs. It is hoped that you will be able to identify an approach that meets your needs and helps TAs/RAs to do their jobs effectively while simultaneously moving them through the graduate program and on to their postgraduate careers.

In the previous chapters, we have taken you from the initial contacts with the graduate instructors and researchers through to this chapter on assessment. We are hopeful that, as you have been reading, you have had some time to reflect on the issues and ideas we have presented. It is now time to help you think more specifically about how you might use the ideas in this chapter and the rest of the book. We do so in the next chapter by moving you toward a specific plan for your supervision.

9

Designing a Plan of Action

As you finish reading this volume, we encourage you to pursue further the many questions surrounding effective supervision of teaching assistants (TAs) and research assistants (RAs). Just as instructors must be reflective about their teaching to remain effective, so must supervisors of TAs and RAs reflect upon what they do in order to design and provide adequate supervision. Such reflectiveness is an ongoing process that will be with you each time you prepare to work with a group of TAs/RAs. We hope you will continue to reflect upon what you are doing, make adjustments, and reflect some more. We also realize that many of you picked up this volume and read it because you have a strong need to take action. This chapter is especially for you.

We have provided a variety of guidelines and strategies throughout the book that you might consider in developing your own approach to TA and RA supervision. As you have read it, we trust you have said to yourself, "Now that's a good idea," "Hmm . . . that's interesting," "Ha! That would never work in my situation," or "I need to think more about how I might do that." Anticipating, or hoping for, such reflective thinking as we wrote, we tried to identify important ideas and approaches for you to consider. But our purpose

127

is also much broader—we hope that you will not only think about these ideas but also take specific steps to address some of them in your own ways. So we are now encouraging you to do your own synthesis and, from the ideas presented and the additional ideas they triggered, cull out those that are not useful for your specific case and, more important, identify some ideas that you really are going to use.

We know that at this stage of the process, you may not be able to be thorough and definitive. Nevertheless, we think it is important to get at least some of your initial thoughts down where you can see them and evaluate them as you begin to structure your interactions with TAs and/or RAs. We think of this as your Action Plan. We will assist you by reviewing the steps through which you can move in developing such a plan. You can think about the process in the same way you expect TAs to think about the planning of a course—by identifying specific goals, strategies for meeting those goals, and ways of assessing whether the strategies have been successful in achieving the goals.

Identifying Goals
for Your Supervisory Practices

What do you want to accomplish with your TAs and RAs? Start generally and think about the three to five goals or areas of competency that you want TAs/RAs to achieve. You might answer the question, "How do I want the TAs/RAs that I will supervise to be different as a result of having worked with me?" Obviously, they must acquire the information and skills that TAs/RAs need to fulfill their immediate responsibilities to research or to undergraduate education. Ask yourself, then, "Do I want TAs to learn to lead discussions? Plan a course? Do I want RAs to practice all or some of the steps of the research process? Adhere to the ethics of research? Participate as a member of a research team?" We have provided in Figure 9.1 a form that may be useful to you as you identify your goals.

Your choice of goals depends, of course, on a variety of factors that you have to consider. Among those factors are

Goals	Strategies	Assessment
Goal #1:		
Goal #2:		
Goal #3:		
Goal #4:		
Goal #5:		

Figure 9.1. Supervisory Plan of Action Worksheet

- The graduate students themselves—their needs, backgrounds, abilities, interests, stages of development, and future goals
- You, with your own needs, interests, abilities, responsibilities, time commitments, and so on
- The specific task you are asking TAs or RAs to fulfill in your discipline—the kinds of skills involved, the necessary accountability, the required timelines, and so on
- The context—such things as the university climate and perspective on TAs/RAs, the departmental policies and perspectives, your role and the role of TAs/RAs, and the parameters of the specific course or research project with which TAs/RAs are working

By considering these factors, you should be able to identify goals that are sensitive to the demands of the specific roles, the needs of the TAs/RAs, your own needs, and the overall context in which you will conduct your supervision. Because of the variation of those factors, we cannot begin to suggest which goals are most important. We can reinforce, however, that the act of setting goals should not be taken lightly because these goals will guide you in structuring your supervisory practices—both the specific strategies and the assessment procedures you will use.

Identifying Strategies

Once you have determined the major goals that you want to accomplish, you can begin to think about specific strategies that will help you accomplish them. For each goal, you should identify specific ways that you plan to achieve that goal. In addition, both the goals and the strategies must take into consideration the important factors that come together in the process. So, again, you will make your choices based on

- The specific roles to be fulfilled now and throughout their professional careers
- The individual TAs/RAs
- You as the supervisor
- The context

Now you can ask yourself questions about strategies that help you address the goals and simultaneously remain sensitive to each of these factors—questions such as

- "What is the best strategy to prepare TAs to be interactive during office hours?" (to address the needs of the TA role)
- "What strategy can I use to help RAs develop basic skills for data analysis?" (to address the needs of the RA role)
- How can the TAs/RAs best learn to be systematically reflective about their teaching/research? (future needs of individual TAs/RAs)

- "What strategy can I use to give TAs (or RAs) the independence they need when I have such a strong personal need for control?" (to address your own needs)
- "What strategies can I use to prepare TAs/RAs for their future professional roles when other faculty and administrators in the department are telling them to focus mostly on what they have to do right now?" (to address contextual factors)

The best strategies will be those that address all the factors simultaneously. Clearly, you cannot select strategies that ignore the needs of the roles, offend TAs/RAs, make you feel uncomfortable, or work directly against the culture of your department or institution. Therefore, you try to achieve the best balance possible. At the same time, you have to realize that at some point, you will not be able to satisfy all the needs at once. In these cases, we encourage you to take a little risk and recognize that there are times that you will want to create the need to "flex." Flexing is like stretching that extra little bit. Even though the TAs/RAs may feel a little uncomfortable, you may want them to stretch in their efforts to gain new perspectives or try new approaches. Similarly, as you try some new strategies, you may have to flex in directions that are new to you. Certainly, there will be times when the strategies you choose will be designed to get other faculty and administrators to flex in their thinking about how TAs/RAs can be supervised. We hope you will be creative.

Identifying Forms of Assessment

In Chapter 8, we have discussed the assessment process in detail. Here, we simply want to reiterate that the approach to assessment must be linked directly to the goals and strategies and must reflect your consideration of the roles, the TAs, yourself, and the context. In some way, determine how you will know if you have met the goals you have set and how you will identify which strategies were most useful in moving TAs and RAs toward those goals. A variety of assessment ideas are probably most useful, ranging from collecting informal feedback to more formal assessments of TA/RA performance.

Final Thoughts

Throughout this volume, we have presented ideas, guidelines, and cautionary notes about developing useful supervisory relationships with TAs and RAs. As you plan for your roles as manager, educational model, and mentor of TAs/RAs, we hope you will see how effective performance in each role will enhance the development of the TAs/RAs you supervise. They need and deserve careful management, an effective educational model, and sustained mentoring that fits with their development from senior learner to colleague-in-training to junior colleague. Anything less denigrates teaching and research and impairs succeeding generations of professionals.

We have given you a big task. Clearly, as this volume suggests, successful supervision of a group of TAs or RAs takes time. It takes time to plan, to meet with TAs/RAs as a group, to talk with them individually, to gather data on their performance, and to follow up to ensure their growth toward professionals. Just as important, it takes energy—the energy of constantly having to provide feedback in the most constructive ways, of generating from your own experience strategies that will assist TAs/RAs to be effective, and following up on implementation of those strategies. The challenges of how to become more effective in some ways seem formidable—they are never ending. Yet that is how and why supervision can remain an intellectually engaging activity, and it helps immensely when those around you are supportive and helpful. Therefore, it is important that you prepare carefully, clarify with your administrators what your supervisory plan for TAs/RAs looks like, and indicate what you will need in terms of time and resources. Try to get those around you to be involved in, committed to, and understanding of your efforts. Administrators and colleagues will benefit from understanding your definition of adequate supervision within the context of your specific department. You must also make clear how you see your role in the process fitting into your larger role as a scholar.

When you have the time and the administrative support to do a good job, seeing TAs and RAs develop through your efforts can be one of the most rewarding teaching experiences you will ever have. This kind of thoughtful supervision of TAs and RAs is a high calling.

It is hoped that your administrators will endorse your efforts and recognize the important contributions you can make to the department, the TAs/RAs, the discipline through the development of the next generation of teaching scholars, and your own development through such a comprehensive approach. We hope that you will begin today!

10

Selected References Useful to Supervisors of Graduate Teaching Assistants and Graduate Research Assistants

If you have not been reading previously about teaching assistant (TA)/research assistant (RA) supervision, you may not realize that materials have been developed during the past few years to assist you in your supervisory role. We have selected a very limited list consisting of books, articles, and videotapes that will be useful to supervisors across many disciplines. Although we have endeavored to include specific disciplinary materials, we are very aware that disciplinary associations are publishing books to assist supervisors of TAs and RAs on a frequent basis, and we encourage you to contact your own disciplinary association to determine if it has publications that will be of use to you.

Section 1 includes general resources on supervising TAs and RAs; Section 2 focuses on TA preparation; Section 3 lists materials to assist supervisors of TAs/RAs with issues involved in diversity and the supervision of international TAs. Section 4 contains discipline-specific print and video resources. We hope the materials will be helpful to you in providing glimpses into the ways that others have solved the problems and challenges you are facing.

134

General Resources

Among general resources are books and articles that are particularly helpful for beginning supervisors:

Angelo, T., & Cross, K. P. (1993). *Classroom assessment techniques* (2nd ed.). San Francisco: Jossey-Bass.

This is a compendium of assessment instruments and ideas that can be used to assess student learning and teaching effectiveness in the college classroom.

Bloom, F. E. (1995). Degrees of uncertainty. *Science, 268* (5212), p. 783.

This short editorial article is based on a report by the Committtree on Science, Engineering and Public Policy that recommends changes in graduate education of scientists and engineers.

Boyer, E. L. (1990). *Scholarship reconsidered: Priorities of the professoriate.* Princeton, NJ: The Carnegie Foundation for the Advancement of Teaching.

This landmark publication has been very helpful in assisting college/university faculty to view teaching as a scholarly activity. It provides a context for supervising TAs and includes a chapter on the preparation of the next generation of scholars.

Civikly, J. M. (1992). *Classroom communication: Principles and practice.* Dubuque, IA: William C. Brown.

This book is particularly useful as a resource for your TAs who are striving to improve their communication with undergraduates.

Davidson, C. I., & Ambrose, S. A. (1994). *The new professor's handbook.* Bolton, MA: Anker.

This volume is useful because it focuses on both teaching and research and includes short chapters on supervising TAs and RAs.

Davis, B. G. (1993). *Tools for teaching.* San Francisco: Jossey-Bass.

This fairly new volume is must reading for new TAs, covering most of the issues they will confront with especially helpful strategies for dealing with diverse undergraduates.

Edgerton, R., Hutchings, P., & Quinlan, K. (1991). *The teaching portfolio: Capturing the scholarship in teaching.* Washington, DC: American Association for Higher Education.

Beginning with the concept that teaching is a scholarly act, this book describes the promise, format, and content of a teaching portfolio and describes how to get started using portfolios on your campus. It is especially valuable in assisting TAs to prepare teaching materials for job interviews.

McKeachie, W. J. (1994). *Teaching tips: Strategies, research, and theory for college and university teachers* (9th ed.). Lexington, MA: D. C. Heath.

Now in its ninth edition, the volume is a classic that has served many beginning instructors in higher education over the years.

Powers, B. (1992). *Instructor excellence: Mastering the delivery of training.* San Francisco: Jossey-Bass.

This how-to guide will help both the professional and novice achieve superior results in the classroom. It offers valuable information about how adults learn and suggests ways to begin training in accordance with standards of excellence.

Richlin, L. (Ed.). (1993). *Preparing faculty for the new conceptions of scholarship.* San Francisco: Jossey-Bass.

This volume is particularly useful for helping educators think about the role of graduate education in preparing graduate students for faculty roles in a changing academy.

Schwartz, A. T. (1994). Graduate education in chemistry: More and more about less and less. *Journal of Chemical Education, 71*(11), 949-950.

The author of this article argues that the tendency of chemistry graduate programs to promote specialization fails to introduce graduate students to the breadth of the discipline.

Weimer, M. (1993). *Improving your classroom teaching.* Newbury Park, CA: Sage.

In this book, Weimer dissects the elements of good teaching—enthusiasm, organization, clarity, and content, among others—and shows how you can become a better instructor.

Worthen, B. R., & Gardner, M. K. (1988). *A second look at the relation of research assistantships and research productivity.* (ERIC Document Reproduction Service No. ED 301 100)

Based on a questionnaire study conducted at five universities, this paper reports findings about the nature of research assistantships and their outcomes. Findings are compared to an earlier study conducted in 1971.

Wright, W. A., & Associates. (1995). *Teaching improvement practices: Successful strategies for higher education.* Bolton, MA: Anker.

This book's survey of current national and international teaching improvement practices is immediately useful to anyone who teaches or evaluates teaching performance in higher education. Chapter 10 of the book identifies the elements of successful TA training programs.

Resources on TA Preparation

Allen, R. R., & Rueter, T. (1990). *Teaching assistant strategies: An introduction to college teaching.* Dubuque, IA: Kendall/Hunt.

This is a helpful volume that can be used as a text for a graduate seminar on teaching.

Andrews, J. D. W. (Ed.). (1985). *Strengthening the teaching assistant faculty.* San Francisco: Jossey-Bass.

Representing the early work on TAs, this volume contains significant general, useful advice.

Chism, N. V. N., & Warner, S. B. (Eds.). (1987). *Institutional responsibilities and responses in employment and education of teaching assistants: Readings from a national conference.* Columbus: Ohio State University, Center for Teaching Excellence.

This set of readings emerged from the First National Conference on the Training and Employment of Graduate Teaching Assistants.

The Journal of Graduate Teaching Assistant Development. Stillwater, OK: New Forums Press.

Begun in 1993, this is one of the few journals devoted exclusively to the preparation of TAs. Focused on improved training, employment, and administration of graduate teaching assistant development programs in higher education, the journal is published four times per year.

Lewis, K. G. (1993). *The TA experience: Preparing for multiple roles.* Stillwater, OK: New Forums Press.

This is the set of readings from the 3rd National Conference on TA Training, including research studies as well as practical advice.

Nyquist, J. D., Abbott, R. D., & Wulff, D. H. (Eds.). (1989). *Teaching assistant training in the 1990s.* San Francisco: Jossey-Bass.

This volume on TA preparation provides the reader with thought-provoking articles calling for recognition of the role that the TAship plays in the development of a professional.

Nyquist, J. D., Abbott, R. D., Wulff, D. H., & Sprague, J. (Eds.). (1991). *Preparing the professoriate of tomorrow to teach: Selected readings in TA training.* Dubuque, IA: Kendall/Hunt.

This book of readings contains competitively selected essays from the 2nd National Conference on TA Training and includes transcriptions of presentations given by Ernest Boyer, K. Patricia Cross, James Anderson, Barbara Solomon, and Wilbert McKeachie.

Two videotapes that provide useful background information on TA training are:

Jamil, S. (Producer & Director). (1993). *What students want* [Videotape, 24 minutes]. (Contact: The Derek Bok Center for Teaching and Learning, Harvard University.)

Based on student interviews, this videotape focuses on factors that facilitate or impede teaching effectiveness of graduate student teaching fellows (TAs).

Quigley, B. (Producer). (1985). *The role of the graduate teaching assistant* [Videotape, 37 minutes]. (Contact: Center for Instructional Development and Research, 109 Parrington Hall, DC-07, University of Washington, Seattle, WA 98195.)

This videotape explores five of the most common responsibilities of graduate students in their roles as TAs: lecturing, leading discussion, directing lab, grading, and tutoring.

Diversity and International
Teaching Assistant Preparation Issues

Bauer, G., & Tanner, M. (Eds.). (1994). *Current approaches to international TA preparation in higher education: A collection of program descriptions.* Seattle, WA: Center for Instructional Development and Research, University of Washington.

This collection describes 48 programs for international TAs at U.S. institutions and includes an overview of program features and informative descriptions of the variety of program formats.

Border, L. L. B., & Chism, N. V. N. (1992). *Teaching for diversity.* San Francisco: Jossey-Bass.

Chapters in this volume address cultural inclusion in the classroom, diverse learning styles, equitable participation in classes, creating multicultural classrooms, feminist classrooms, and portraits of classroom diversity programs at eight universities.

Communicating across cultures. (1987). [Videotape, 30 minutes]. (Contact: Copeland and Griggs Productions, 302 23rd Avenue, San Francisco, CA 94121.)

The video addresses assumptions in communication through 12 vignettes of typical misunderstandings that occur when people communicate across cultures. Communication settings shown include negotiating, selling, and managing conflict. The examples illustrate possible causes of miscommunication and suggest how individuals can become more aware and adapt their communication in recognition of different cultural communication styles.

Davis, C. H. (Director), & Lambert, E. J. (Producer). (1990). *Making a difference: Teaching for black student retention* [Videotape, 24 minutes]. (Contact: Faculty and TA Development, Ohio State University, 20 Lord Hall, 124 West 17th Avenue, Columbus, OH 43214.)

The film covers problems that black students face at universities and provides insights into why, although academically prepared, many black students leave college. Topics such as alienation in the classroom, racial stereotyping, the omission of black history, and some faculty attitudes are discussed. The film ends on a positive note with suggestions for improvement.

Kurashice, L. Y., Elenes, A., & Hibbard, K. (Producers). (1989). *It does happen here.* [Videotape, 18 minutes]. Madison: University of Wisconsin.

The video depicts examples of racism on campus and then moves to a group of minority students discussing personal experiences of racism. The students offer suggestions for improvement while recognizing that there is no simple formula and that fighting racism is a constant process of educating each other.

Madden, C. G., & Myers, C. L. (Eds.). (1994). *Discourse and performance of international teaching assistants.* Alexandria, VA: TESOL.

This comprehensive volume presents specific issues related to the language needs of international TAs. Implications of these language needs for ITAs' classroom teaching are addressed, and pedagogical suggestions are offered.

Quigley, B. (Producer). (1991). *Teaching in the diverse classroom.* [Videotape, 37 minutes]. (Contact: Center for Instructional Development and Research, 109 Parrington Hall, DC-07, University of Washington, Seattle, WA 98195.)

This video identifies four strategies that faculty and TAs can use to teach effectively in classrooms that include students from diverse backgrounds. Students discuss their educational experiences, and teachers explain how they adapt their teaching so that all students feel included and are challenged to learn.

Roberts, H., Gonzales, J. C., Harris, O. D., Huff, D. J., Johns, A. M., Lou, R., & Scott, O. L. (1994). *Teaching from a multicultural perspective.* Thousand Oaks, CA: Sage.

This volume offers a broad repertoire of approaches that instructors can use to teach a culturally diverse student population. These approaches range from instructional strategies to curriculum transformation and assessment tools.

Schoem, D., Frankel, L., Zúñiga, X., & Lewis, E. A. (1993). *Multicultural teaching in the university.* Westport, CT: Praeger.

This book offers many examples of experiences in a variety of disciplines. There are sections covering courses on intergroup relations and on racism, sexism, and diversity, and general courses giving attention to diversity. Additional sections cover teacher training and nonformal education, the insiders' critique of multicultural teaching, and questions and responses on multicultural teaching and conflict in the classroom.

Discipline Specific Publications on TA/RA Preparation

Campbell, F. L., Blalock, H. M., Jr., & McGee, R. (1985). *Teaching sociology: The quest for excellence*. Chicago: Nelson-Hall.

Case, B. A., & Blackwelder, M. A. (1992). The graduate student cohort, doctoral department expectations, and teaching preparation. *American Mathematical Society Notices, 39*(5), 412-418.

Ellis, A. B. (1993). *Teaching general chemistry: A materials science companion*. York, PA: American Chemical Society.

Gustafson, M. (Ed.). (1991). *Becoming a historian: A survival guide for women and men*. Washington, DC: American Historical Association.

Krantz, S. G. (1993). *How to teach mathematics: A personal perspective*. Providence, RI: American Mathematical Society.

Lumsden, E. A., et al. (1988). Preparation of graduate students as classroom teachers and supervisors in applied and research settings. *Teaching of Psychology, 5*, 21-23.

Nyquist, J. D., & Wulff, D. H. (Eds.). (1992). *Preparing teaching assistants for instructional roles: Supervising TAs in communication*. Annandale, VA: Speech Communication Association.

Rickard, H. C., et al. (1991). Teaching of psychology: A required course for all doctoral students. *Teaching of Psychology, 18*, 235-236.

Thinking together: Collaborative learning in science. (1992). [Videotape, 18 minutes]. (Contact: The Derek Bok Center for Teaching and Learning, Harvard University.)

Three science classes at Harvard varying in size from a large lecture class to a small section are featured (introductory physics, astronomy, and a chemistry quiz section), with instructors stressing student involvement in the learning process.

Walz, J. C. (Ed.). (1992). *Development and supervision of teaching assistants in foreign languages*. Boston: Heinle & Heinle.

Wankat, P. C., & Oreovicz, F. S. (1993). *Teaching engineering*. New York: McGraw-Hill.

References

Allen, D., & Ryan, K. (1969). *Microteaching*. Reading, MA: Addison-Wesley.

Anderson, E. (Ed.). (1993). *Campus use of the teaching portfolio: Twenty-five profiles*. Washington, DC: American Association for Higher Education.

Angelo, T. A., & Cross, P. (1993). *Classroom assessment techniques: A handbook for college teachers* (2nd ed.). San Francisco: Jossey-Bass.

Austin, A. E. (1992). Supporting the professor as teacher: The Lilly Teaching Fellows Program. *Review of Higher Education, 16*(1), 85-106.

Austin, A. E. (1993). Emerging lesson on how faculty develop as teachers. In M. Weimer (Ed.), *Faculty as teachers: Taking stock of what we know* (pp. 9-11). University Park, PA: National Center on Postsecondary Teaching, Learning, and Assessment.

Bauer, G. (1992). *Instructional communication concerns of international teaching assistants*. Unpublished doctoral dissertation, Pennsylvania State University, University Park, PA.

Boice, R. (1991). New faculty as teachers. *Journal of Higher Education, 62*, 150-173.

Boice, R. (1992). *The new faculty member: Supporting and fostering professional development*. San Francisco: Jossey-Bass.

Bondeson, W. B. (1992). Faculty development and the new American scholar. *To Improve the Academy, 11*, 3-12.

Book, C., & Eisenberg, E. M. (1979, November). *Communication concerns of graduate and undergraduate teaching assistants*. Paper presented at the annual meeting of the Speech Communication Association, San Antonio, TX.

Braskamp, L. A., & Ory, J. C. (1994). *Assessing faculty work: Enhancing individual and institutional performance*. San Francisco: Jossey-Bass.

Bresnahan, M. I., & Kim, M. S. (1991, May). *The effect of authoritarianism in bias toward foreign teaching assistants*. Paper delivered at the 41st annual meeting of the International Communication Association, Intercultural Division, Chicago.

141

Brookfield, S. D. (1990). *The skillful teacher.* San Francisco: Jossey-Bass.

Chism, N. (1988, April). *The process of development in college teachers: Toward a model.* Paper presented at the annual meeting of the American Educational Research Association, New Orleans.

Chism, N. (1993). How faculty develop teaching expertise. In M. Weimer (Ed.), *Faculty as teachers: Taking stock of what we know* (pp. 33-36). University Park, PA: National Center on Postsecondary Teaching, Learning, and Assessment.

Darling, A. L. (1986, November). *On becoming a graduate student: An examination of communication in the socialization process.* Paper presented at the annual meeting of the Speech Communication Association, Chicago.

Darling, A. L. (1992). Preparing TAs for student diversity. In J. D. Nyquist & D. H. Wulff (Eds.), *Preparing teaching assistants for instructional roles: Supervising TAs in communication.* Annandale, VA: Speech Communication Association.

Duba-Beiderman, L. (1993). Graduate assistant development: Problems of role ambiguity and faculty supervision. In K. G. Lewis (Ed.), *The TA experience: Preparing for multiple roles* (pp. 7-13). Stillwater, OK: New Forums Press.

Edgerton, R., Hutchings, P., & Quinlan, K. (1991). *The teaching portfolio: Capturing the scholarship in teaching.* Washington, DC: American Association for Higher Education.

Fink, L. D. (Ed.). (1984). *The first year of college teaching.* San Francisco: Jossey-Bass.

Fuller, F. F. (1969). Concerns of teachers: A developmental perspective. *American Educational Research Journal, 2,* 207-226.

Grossman, P. L. (1992). What models matter: An alternative view on professional growth in teaching. *Review of Educational Research, 62,* 171-179.

Hudson-Ross, S., & Dong, Y. R. (1990). Literacy learning as a reflection of language and culture: Chinese elementary school education. *The Reading Teacher, 44,* 110-123.

Hunt, D. (1971). *Matching models in education.* Toronto: Ontario Institute for Studies in Education.

Hutchings, P. (1993). Introducing faculty portfolios: Early lessons from CUNY York College: A case study. *AAHE Bulletin, 45*(9), 14-17.

Jenrette, M. (1993). How do faculty develop as teachers? Ask a teacher. In M. Weimer (Ed.), *Faculty as teachers: Taking stock of what we know* (pp. 67-69). University Park, PA: National Center on Postsecondary Teaching, Learning, and Assessment.

Kagan, D. M. (1988). Research on the supervision of counselors—and teachers—in training: Linking two bodies of literature. *Review of Educational Research, 58,* 1-24.

Kugel, P. (1993). How professors develop as teachers. *Studies in Higher Education, 3,* 315-328.

Meyers, C. (1986). *Teaching students to think critically.* San Francisco: Jossey-Bass.

Myers, C. L. (1994). Question-based discourse in science labs: Issues for ITAs. In C. G. Madden & C. L. Myers (Eds.), *Discourse and performance of international teaching assistants* (pp. 83-102). Alexandria, VA: TESOL.

Nelson, G. (1991). Effective teaching behavior for international teaching assistants. In J. D. Nyquist, R. D. Abbott, D. H. Wulff, & J. Sprague (Eds.), *Preparing the professoriate of tomorrow to teach: Selected readings in TA training* (pp. 427-434). Dubuque, IA: Kendall/Hunt.

Nelson, G. L. (1992). The relationship between the use of personal, cultural examples in international teaching assistants' lectures and uncertainty reduction, student attitude, student recall, and ethnocentrism. *International Journal of Intercultural Relations, 16*, 33-52.

Nyquist, J. D. (1993). The development of faculty as teachers. In M. Weimer (Ed.), *Faculty as teachers: Taking stock of what we know* (pp. 89-94). University Park, PA: National Center on Postsecondary Teaching, Learning, and Assessment.

Nyquist, J., Skow, L., Sprague, J., & Wulff, D. (1991, November). *Research on stages of teaching assistant development.* Paper presented at the Third National Conference on TA Training, Austin, TX.

Nyquist, J., & Sprague, J. (1992). Developmental stages of TAs. In J. Nyquist & D. Wulff (Eds.), *Preparing teaching assistants for instructional roles: Supervising TAs in communication.* Washington, DC: Speech Communication Association.

Nyquist, J. D., & Staton-Spicer, A. Q. (1987). Non-traditional intervention strategies for improving the teaching effectiveness of graduate teaching assistants. *To Improve the Academy, 6*, 168-182.

Nyquist, J. D., & Wulff, D. H. (Eds.). (1992). *Preparing teaching assistants for instructional roles: Supervising TAs in communication.* Annandale, VA: Speech Communication Association.

Ory, J. C., & Ryan, K. E. (1993). *Tips for improving testing and grading.* Newbury Park, CA: Sage.

Pica, T., Barnes, A., & Finger, A. (1990). *Teaching matters: Skills and strategies for international teaching assistants.* New York: Newbury House.

Powers, B. (1992). *Instructor excellence: Mastering the delivery of training.* San Francisco: Jossey-Bass.

Prawat, R. S. (1989). Teaching for understanding: Three key attributes. *Teaching & Teacher Education, 5*(4), 315-328.

Resnick, L. B. (1989). Introduction. In L. B. Resnick (Ed.), *Knowing, learning, and instruction: Essays in honor of Robert Glaser* (pp. 1-24). Hillsdale, NJ: Lawrence Erlbaum.

Samberg, T., Wiegand, D., & Selfe, S. (1993). Course-specific resource manual for chemistry laboratory courses. In K. G. Lewis (Ed.), *The TA experience: Preparing for multiple roles* (pp. 232-237). Stillwater, OK: New Forums Press.

Scardamalia, M., & Bereiter, C. (1985). Fostering the development of self-regulation in children's knowledge processing. In S. Chipman, W. Segal, & R. Glaser (Eds.), *Thinking and learning skills: Vol. 2. Research and open questions* (pp. 361-385). Hillsdale, NJ: Lawrence Erlbaum.

Schön, D. A. (1987). *Educating the reflective practitioner: Toward a new design for teaching and learning in the professions.* San Francisco: Jossey-Bass.

Seldin, P. (1985). *Changing practices in faculty evaluation.* San Francisco: Jossey-Bass.

Seldin, P. (1991). *The teaching portfolio: A practical guide to improved performance and promotion/tenure decisions.* Bolton, MA: Anker.

Seldin, P., & Associates. (1993). *Successful use of teaching portfolios.* Bolton, MA: Anker.

Smith, R. M., Byrd, P., Nelson, G. L., Barrett, R. P., & Constantinides, J. C. (1992). *Crossing pedagogical oceans: International teaching assistants in U.S. undergraduate education* (ASHE-ERIC Higher Education Report No. 8). Washington,

DC: George Washington University, School of Education and Human Development.

Sorcinelli, M. D., & Austin, A. E. (Eds.). (1992). *Developing new and junior faculty.* San Francisco: Jossey-Bass.

Sprague, J., & Nyquist, J. D. (1989). TA supervision. In J. D. Nyquist, R. D. Abbott, & D. H. Wulff (Eds.), *Teaching assistant training in the 1990s* (pp. 37-53). San Francisco: Jossey-Bass.

Sprague, J., & Nyquist, J. D. (1991). A developmental perspective on the TA role. In J. D. Nyquist, R. D. Abbott, D. H. Wulff, & J. Sprague (Eds.), *Preparing the professoriate of tomorrow to teach: Selected readings in TA training* (pp. 295-312). Dubuque, IA: Kendall/Hunt.

Sprinthall, N. A., & Theis-Sprinthall, L. (1983). The need for theoretical frameworks in educating teachers: A cognitive developmental perspective. In K. R. Howey & W. E. Gardner (Eds.), *The education of teachers: A look ahead.* New York: Longmans.

Staton, A. Q., & Darling, A. L. (1989). Socialization of teaching assistants. In J. D. Nyquist, R. D. Abbott, & D. H. Wulff (Eds.), *Teaching assistant training in the 1990s* (pp. 15-22). San Francisco: Jossey-Bass.

Staton-Spicer, A. Q., & Bassett, R. E. (1979). Communication concerns of preservice and inservice elementary school teachers. *Human Communication Research, 5,* 138-146.

Stoltenberg, C. (1981). Approaching supervision from a developmental perspective: The counselor complexity model. *Journal of Counseling Psychology, 28,* 59-65.

Tanner, M. W., Selfe, S., & Wiegand, D. (1993). The balanced equation to training chemistry ITAs. In K. G. Lewis (Ed.), *The TA experience: Preparing for multiple roles* (pp. 410-419). Stillwater, OK: New Forums Press.

Teaching in America: A guide for international faculty. (1993). [Videotape, 38 minutes]. Harvard Teaching Series, The Derek Bok Center for Teaching and Learning, Harvard University.

Tierney, W. G., & Rhoads, R. A. (1994). *Faculty socialization as cultural process: A mirror of institutional commitment* (ASHE/ERIC Higher Education Report No. 93-6). Washington, DC: George Washington University, School of Education and Human Development.

Weimer, M. (1993a). How faculty develop as teachers: Themes in variation. In M. Weimer (Ed.), *Faculty as teachers: Taking stock of what we know* (pp. 127-131). University Park, PA: National Center on Postsecondary Teaching, Learning, and Assessment.

Weimer, M. (1993b). *Improving your classroom teaching.* Newbury Park, CA: Sage.

Williams, J. M. (1986, November). *Hidden meanings: Critical thinking and acculturation.* Paper presented at the University of Chicago Conference on Cognition and Writing in Discourse Communities, Chicago.

Wulff, D. H. (1993). Tales of transformation: Applying a teaching effectiveness perspective to stories about teaching. *Communication Education, 42*(4), 377-397.

About the Authors

Jody D. Nyquist is Director of the Center for Instructional Development and Research (CIDR) and a faculty member in the Department of Speech Communication at the University of Washington. Her interest in instructional communication has led to exploring how one becomes a teaching scholar in higher education, and thus to a focus on the TA/RA experience. She has coedited three volumes and has written numerous articles on various aspects of TA development and TA preparation. Currently, she is Principal Investigator for a four-year, longitudinal study looking at TA development at the Universities of Washington, Michigan State, and San Jose State. The study is being funded by PEW Charitable Trusts and the Spencer Foundation.

She has presented on the topic of TA/RA development and supervision at numerous universities across the United States and in Israel, Saudi Arabia, Australia, and New Zealand, where she served as a Fulbright Senior Scholar in 1992. In December 1994, she keynoted the first British National Conference, "Using Graduate Teaching Assistants Effectively," at the University of Warwick in the United Kingdom.

Donald H. Wulff is the Associate Director of the Center for Instructional Development and Research at the University of Washington, where he coordinates the TA training services provided to departments through the center. During the past 15 years, he has developed extensive experience through consulting with faculty members, TAs, and TA supervisors on the preparation of TAs and RAs. He has presented hundreds of workshops and seminars, both on his own campus and across the country, and has coedited three volumes on TA training. His recent research has focused on stages of TA development and approaches for preparing TAs for their instructional roles. Currently, he sits on the editorial board of *The Journal of Graduate Teaching Assistant Development.*

For the past 6 years, he has been involved in the leadership of the Professional and Organizational Development Network in Higher Education (POD), which focuses on improvement of higher education through faculty, instructional, and organizational development, and he served as president in 1993–1994. He has taught a variety of university courses in communication, and in 1984, he was a recipient of the Distinguished Teaching Award at the University of Washington.

Gabriele Bauer, Ph.D., received her graduate degree at Penn State in speech communication with emphases on English as a Second Language and instructional supervision. Her research interests focus on the adjustment of international graduate students to the U.S. university setting, the development of their intercultural sensitivity, and their instructional concerns and approaches. As an Instructional Development Specialist at CIDR, Dr. Bauer is a consultant in the ITA Program, and she consults also with faculty and TAs from a wide variety of disciplines on issues of instructional improvement and program evaluation.